Foreword

by the Home Secretary,
the Rt Hon David Blunkett MP

We have a tradition of living in a free and open society and we are used to taking people at face value – trusting them to be who they say they are.

Recent events have brought home how, in today's rapidly changing world, the need for trust and confidence actually require us to move beyond this and take the opportunity of new biometric technology which allows for a completely new level of verifying identity.

The threat of global terrorism, the ease with which large numbers of people now travel around the world, and the proliferation of identity fraud make secure identification more vital than ever.

We all need greater certainty about whether people are who they say they are - whether travelling, or in business, or in ensuring that free public services are accessed only by those who are entitled. Not only that, but we are right to expect greater security and protection of our own identity. That is why there has been a steadily growing interest in the introduction of identity cards in the United Kingdom – and a growing recognition that, rather than threatening our vital freedoms, they would actually help preserve them.

Following a public consultation, I announced in November the Government's decision to build a base for a compulsory national identity cards scheme. I made clear then that we would proceed by incremental steps, building first on existing, widely held voluntary identity documents, and only taking a final decision later to move to compulsion. Eventually everyone lawfully resident in the UK would be required to register for a card – but there would be no compulsion to carry the card or to produce it without good reason. This move to compulsion would only happen once the initial stage of the scheme had proved to be successful and following a further debate and the approval of both Houses of Parliament.

Although the process will build on existing documents, such as passports and driving licences, we need a clear additional legal framework before we can introduce a national identity cards scheme.

The next step is therefore to publish, for consultation, our proposals for legislation in the draft Identity Cards Bill. That is the purpose of this document. I want us to be able to test and refine these proposals before legislation is introduced finally into Parliament.

I am inviting general views as well as specific drafting comments on our legislative proposals. In particular, I am looking forward to receiving comments from the House of Commons Home Affairs Select Committee which has been undertaking an inquiry on Identity Cards and is set to carry out pre-legislative scrutiny of the draft Identity Cards Bill. We will take full account of all the comments we receive before going ahead with the legislation.

I want everyone who is living lawfully in the UK to be able to assert his or her true identity and to protect that identity against fraud, as well as protecting their freedoms against new threats from global terrorism and organised crime. The scheme we are building will do this – but I want to work with all interested parties to make sure we get it right.

UHI
Millennium
Institute

Please return/renew this item by the last date shown

Tillibh/ath-chlaraidh seo ron cheann-latha mu dheireadh

by Command of Her Majesty
April 2004

CM 6178

£16.10

Contents

ANNEXES

Executive summary

1. The Government announced on 11th November 2003 its proposal to build the base for a compulsory national identity cards scheme. This was set out in Identity Cards: The Next Steps (Cm 6020). The Government is now seeking, through this consultation, comments on a proposed Identity Cards Bill that would establish the legislative framework for the incremental introduction of this scheme.

2. This consultation paper explains (at Chapter 1) the need for new legislation. New legislation is required to establish a clear legal foundation for what is a major policy development and also to provide a statutory basis for spending public money on setting up the scheme and charging the fees required to recover the cost of issuing cards. The legislation will also ensure that organisations issuing cards have powers to conduct more rigorous checks on applicants so as to guard against identity fraud. It will provide safeguards for individuals who are issued with identity cards to ensure that their information is held securely as well as introducing new offences on the possession of false or improperly obtained identity documents.

3. The draft Bill is an enabling measure. It will set out a clear framework for the identity cards scheme, which will cover everyone aged 16 or over who is legally resident in the United Kingdom for 3 months or more. As with any project of this size and complexity there is a great deal of development work to be done before it is possible to finalise all the operational details, including the precise technical arrangements for recording biometric identifiers such as facial image, finger scans and iris images, which will provide a way of uniquely confirming the identity of cardholders. Accordingly, many of the detailed provisions (such as fee levels or the procedure for making an application) are not yet settled and will be laid out later in Regulations.

4. The 41 draft clauses and 2 schedules for the Identity Cards Bill are printed at Annex A. Annex B includes explanatory notes on the draft clauses and Annex C provides information on the regulatory and race impact assessments. Annex D sets out how the draft Bill will ensure that the Identity Cards scheme complies with the Data Protection Act 1998.

5.   The main features of the draft Identity Cards Bill are as follows (a fuller summary can be found in Chapter 2 of the consultation paper):

- Setting up a National Identity Register that will include all the identity information held on those individuals who have been registered and issued with an identity card;
- Establishing powers to issue identity cards including "plain" cards as well as a power to designate existing documents (such as passport or driving licence cards) as identity cards;
- Data sharing powers to ensure that the issuing authority is able to check the details provided by an applicant against information already held on other databases. This provision will ensure that biographical checks can be made against other government databases to confirm the applicant's identity and guard against fraud;
- Providing reassurance that disclosure of information from the National Identity Register without the individual's consent will not be allowed, apart from in specified exceptional circumstances, such as on grounds of national security or for the prevention or investigation of crime;
- Establishing new criminal offences for the possession of false identity documents. These will cover offences relating to the new identity card as well as existing identity documents that are false or have been improperly obtained;
- Powers to set a date when it would become compulsory to register and be issued with a card (but not compulsory to carry a card which is specifically prohibited in the draft Bill). This provision could be brought in only once the initial stage of the identity cards scheme was in place and following a vote in both Houses of Parliament on a detailed report which sets out all the reasons for the proposed move to compulsion;
- A provision that would enable Regulations to be made, once it was compulsory to register and hold an identity card, to make it a requirement to provide proof of identity by the production of an identity card to access public services.

6.   There are a number of wider issues mentioned in the consultation paper (at Chapter 3) that do not require legislation and so are not covered in the draft Bill. These include the arrangements for the organisational structure and governance of the card issuing process as well as details that will be set out in Regulations such as the technical specification for cards. The paper also explains the proposed incremental approach for building towards a compulsory national identity cards scheme - as originally set out in "Identity cards: the Next Steps" – first building on existing identity documents, and only once the conditions are right moving to the second stage of the scheme in which it would be compulsory to register. The paper also sets out some of the reasons for introducing identity cards, and reports on relevant international developments relating for example to the inclusion of biometrics on passports.

7.   Chapter 4 of the paper lists the consultation points. Comments are sought on the draft
      legislation from individuals and organisations. The House of Commons Select Committee on
      Home Affairs will, in addition, be carrying out formal pre-legislative scrutiny of the draft Bill.
      The Government will take account of all comments on the draft Identity Cards Bill before it
      takes a decision to introduce substantive legislation on identity cards into Parliament which
      would be once parliamentary time allows.

8.   Any comments should be sent **by Tuesday 20th July 2004** to: -

      Robin Woodland
      Legislation Consultation
      Identity Cards Programme
      Home Office
      3rd Floor
      Allington Towers
      19 Allington Street
      London SW1E 5EB

9.   Comments may also be sent by fax to: 020 7035 5386 or by e-mail to: -
      identitycards@homeoffice.gsi.gov.uk including the words "consultation response" in the
      subject title.

Chapter 1

INTRODUCTION

The consultation on Identity Cards legislation

1.1   The Government is proposing to build the base for a compulsory national identity cards scheme and announced on 11th November 2003 its decision to introduce an identity cards scheme on an incremental basis. A summary of the proposals was set out in **Identity Cards: The Next Steps** (Cm 6020) published on the same day. It was announced subsequently in the Queen's speech at the opening of Parliament on 26th November 2003 that a draft Identity Cards Bill would be published during 2004. **This paper now sets out for consultation the Government's plans for legislation on identity cards and includes the text of draft clauses of an Identity Cards Bill.**

1.2   The Government is convinced that a national identity cards scheme will bring major benefits, but given the size and the complexity of introducing a national identity cards scheme there will be no "big bang" approach. There are a number of practical issues that can only be resolved in the years ahead and it has therefore been decided that it would be best to proceed by incremental steps with the introduction of the first identity cards, on current plans, starting in **2007-08**.

1.3   Although a decision has already been made on the **principle** of introducing identity cards, the Government has made clear that it wishes to consult on the details of proposed legislation. Comments are therefore now sought from organisations as well as from individuals on the scope and contents of the draft legislation.

1.4   The House of Commons Home Affairs Select Committee is carrying out an inquiry on all aspects of identity cards. In addition the Committee is to undertake formal pre-legislative scrutiny of the draft Identity Cards Bill. This is expected to include taking evidence on the Government's legislative proposals before publishing the Committee's own views on the draft legislation.

1.5   The draft clauses for the Identity Cards Bill are attached at **Annex A**, together with a draft set of explanatory notes on the clauses at **Annex B**. **Annex C** discusses the issues that will affect any regulatory impact assessments on how the scheme might be used. It also includes a discussion of the main factors to consider in the race equality impact assessment. **Annex D** sets out how the draft Bill complies with the Data Protection Act 1998.

The need for legislation

1.6   The reason for introducing legislation on identity cards now is to ensure that there is a clear legal basis for such a major policy development. Whilst the costs of the identity cards scheme will be recovered from fee income, there needs to be a statutory basis for spending public money on establishing the scheme. Legislative powers are also needed to be able to set the fees required to recover the cost of issuing cards and to ensure that organisations issuing cards have powers to conduct more rigorous checks on applicants to guard against identity fraud.

1.7   The draft Bill sets out a legal framework for the scheme and enshrines certain key protections (e.g. against "function creep" or unauthorised access to the National Identity Register database) in primary legislation.

1.8   The Bill proposed is an **enabling** measure that will set out a clear framework for the identity cards scheme. Many of the detailed provisions (for example the level of fees and the exact process needed to make an application) will be set out in Regulations later, rather than in the Bill itself. Establishing these arrangements in Regulations is not simply a matter of convenience or timing, but is necessary so that details of processes such as changes to fees or application forms can be amended over the life of the scheme.

1.9   Similarly, detailed arrangements for issuing cards will not be set out in the draft Bill, in order to allow potential suppliers of systems for issuing identity cards the freedom to propose innovative and flexible solutions, within the clear legal framework we have set out, thereby ensuring value for money.

1.10   There will of course be an opportunity for further scrutiny of the detailed provisions at a later stage. Regulations made under the Bill will be laid before Parliament and where there are any important issues to be decided the Regulations will be debated in Parliament and approved formally by a resolution of both the House of Commons and the House of Lords.

1.11   We will proceed in two stages. The **first stage**, now that the Office of Government Commerce (OGC) has confirmed that the programme is ready to proceed, is to publish draft legislation to enable the scheme to be introduced and pave the way for the establishment of more reliable means of proving people's identity. This will include: –

(i)   establishing a National Identity Register;

(ii)   proceeding towards more secure passports and driving licences based on biometric technology – with personalised, specific identifiers;

(iii)   for those who do not need a passport or driving licence and choose to take it up, making available a voluntary plain identity card. This would not, of course, become compulsory (or be mandatory for access to services) until the appropriate further Parliamentary decision – see below;

(iv)   introducing mandatory biometric identity documents for foreign nationals coming to stay in the UK for longer than 3 months. For nationals from countries in the European Economic Area[1] (EEA) this will be done in a way which is fully compatible with European law.

1.12   If the conditions were right, this first stage phased roll-out could then be followed by the **second stage**, a move to a compulsory card scheme in which it would be compulsory to have a card – though not to carry one – and to produce a card to access public services in ways defined by those services. In the case of those services for which the devolved administrations have responsibility, decisions on production of a card to access those services would be a matter for them.

1.13   The move to compulsion would require full debate and a vote in both Houses of Parliament. Clearly the Government would only take this step after a rigorous evaluation of the first stage, when it was confident that everything was in place to enable the scheme to work successfully, that its benefits outweighed any costs and risks and that it was fully affordable within future agreed spending plans. In particular, we would want to be confident that: -

•   roll out during the first phase has already delivered significant coverage of the population;

[1] The European Economic Area (EEA) comprises the 25 EU member states following enlargement on 1st May 2004 together with Norway, Iceland and Liechtenstein. Although not a member of the EEA, similar rights of free movement apply to nationals of Switzerland.

- there is clear public acceptance for the principle of a compulsory ID card which would be used to access free public services. This would already have included a scheme of charges based on cost recovery and subsidy for those on low incomes; use of the card for access to free public services would not prevent people without cards from accessing emergency services, and those on low incomes and other vulnerable groups would not be disadvantaged;
- the scheme would make a further significant difference to tackling fraudulent access to free public services, and to tackling illegal working at an acceptable compliance cost to business; and
- the technology is working and public services have implemented the technology and business changes necessary to take full advantage of the scheme.

1.14   Before any move could be made to the second stage of the identity cards scheme (when it would become compulsory to register and be issued with a card), the Government would produce a report setting out its case for the move to compulsion and covering all relevant aspects of the proposal. This report would be laid before Parliament to allow for a period of considered reflection and would then be put before both Houses inviting them to debate and approve the Government's proposition in the report. If the report were approved the Government could then lay an order for further parliamentary approval to set a date when it would become compulsory to register.

1.15   Details of the specific consultation points on the draft Identity Cards Bill and where to send comments are set out in Section 4 (paragraphs 4.6 to 4.12) and **all comments are requested to arrive by Tuesday 20th July 2004**.

Chapter 2

PROPOSALS FOR LEGISLATION ON IDENTITY CARDS

Scope of the Identity Cards Bill

2.1 Proposals for legislation are set out in the draft Identity Cards Bill at **Annex A**. The draft Bill will provide the legislative framework to enable a national identity cards scheme to be established so that individuals can easily prove their identity, including their nationality and immigration status. It does so by establishing the National Identity Register and defining as an "ID card" for the purposes of the draft Bill a card which is either designated as such or is issued by the Secretary of State and links to an individual's entry on the Register.

2.2 The Bill will:

- establish a database - the **National Identity Register**, which will hold identity details of those people registered and issued with a card;
- specify **information that may be recorded in the Register** (including the biometric data) and the safeguards to ensure this is only available to those with lawful authority;
- provide **data-sharing powers** to conduct thorough background checks on applicants for identity cards so as to make sure that the details they have provided are correct;
- establish **powers to issue identity cards**. This includes designating existing documents (which could include passport cards, residence permits for foreign nationals, and photocard driving licences) as part of the identity cards scheme. It also includes the power to issue 'plain' biometric identity cards;
- enable **Regulations** to be made that will specify how an application for an identity card should be made and the information that must be produced to support an application;
- set out the safeguards to protect an individual's data and define the exceptional circumstances in which specified agencies, such as security and intelligence agencies and law enforcement agencies could have **information disclosed from the Register** without an individual's consent;

- provide safeguards over "**function creep**" in terms of information that may be held on the card or the Register;
- enable public and private sector organisations to **verify a person's identity by checking a card** against the National Identity Register, with the person's consent, to validate identity and residential status before providing services;
- create new **criminal offences around the misuse of identity cards and other identity fraud issues** and provide a civil penalty for failure to notify changes affecting the accuracy of an individual's entry on the Register;
- include enabling powers so that in the future **Regulations can be made relating to the use of the card scheme**; and
- provide a power to **set a date when the scheme would become compulsory** with a requirement to register and be issued with a card and a civil penalty for failure to register.

2.3   The Bill will provide enabling powers to establish the identity cards scheme. Many of the detailed arrangements for the card scheme will be determined as the identity cards programme proceeds and the systems for issuing identity cards are designed and procured. These detailed arrangements will be set out in regulations made using secondary legislation provided for in the draft Identity Cards Bill. This would include the exact format of applications and the levels of fees to be charged.

National Identity Register

2.4   The draft Bill at Clauses 1-3 establishes a **National Identity Register**. This will hold all the information held about those people who have registered and been issued with an identity card.

2.5   It will be a new register that will be created as people apply for identity cards. It will **not** be simply a revised or updated version of existing databases, for example of persons issued with passports or driving licences.

2.6   Clause 1(2) sets out the statutory purposes of the Register. It makes clear that the Register is to provide a record of "registrable facts" about the identity of individuals who are resident in the United Kingdom or have applied to be entered on the register. This will facilitate the issue of identity cards as well as providing a system for verification of the identity of registered people with their consent. Disclosure of information otherwise from the Register will be strictly controlled. Unlike, for example electoral registers, the National Identity Register will **not** be open for any general access or inspection.

2.7   "Registrable facts" include, as spelt out at Clause 1(3), identity information, such as names, date of birth, place of residence, other or previous addresses, nationality and, where relevant, immigration status and conditions of stay in the United Kingdom. It will also include an audit log of when information on the Register has been accessed. Although there are no plans for it at this stage, the Bill would also allow voluntary information, recorded at the individual's own request. The Government would need to decide whether to bring this facility into effect and would specify the type of voluntary information that might be included if it was likely to be of benefit to cardholders (for example emergency information such as blood group or organ donor status).

2.8   In order to clarify and set out clear limits for the information to be held on the Register, Clause 3(1) specifies that apart from technical and administrative data, the information that will be held on the National Identity Register must be as specified in the draft Bill at Schedule 1. It includes information that is likely to be printed on the face of an identity card (e.g. name or date of birth) together with other information (such as a PIN or audit log) that would be held on the database but not shown on the card.

2.9   The Schedule lists the categories of information that **may** be held on the Register, although not every item listed need be included when the Register is established. The Schedule includes the following information: -

Personal information
- a person's full name and other names which he or she currently or has previously used (e.g. a stage name or maiden name);
- date and place of birth;
- gender;
- address, this will include the person's principal residence together with any other addresses at which they reside.

Identifying information
- a photograph;
- fingerprints or other biometric information such as an iris image.

Residential status
- nationality (if a person holds dual nationality, such as British and Irish, it would be possible for both to be recorded);
- for foreign nationals, immigration status.

Personal reference numbers

- each person will have a "national identity registration number" together with other relevant reference numbers recorded (e.g. national insurance number or existing passport number).

Record history

- previous details (e.g. earlier names or addresses) will be held on the register.

Registration history

- details of previous identity cards or registration applications made by an individual will be retained on the register.

Validation information

- information about any background evidence or document checks carried out to confirm identity or to reconfirm it when re-registering.

Security information

- security information such as an individual's personal identification number (PIN) or a password or other information that enables a person to identify themselves remotely would be held on the Register.

Access records

- there would be an "audit log" held on the Register of each occasion when an individual's identity record has been checked.

2.10   The draft Bill at Clause 3(4) – (6) provides that the list of information in the Schedule may only be added to or amended by laying an order before Parliament that would be subject to the affirmative resolution procedure – that is it would need to be debated and approved by both Houses of Parliament. Any such changes would also need to be consistent with the statutory purposes of the Register and the definition of "registrable facts" in Clause 1(4). This means that categories of information that are **not** related to establishing identity, such as criminal convictions or medical conditions, could not be added by Regulations.

2.11   Anyone entered on the Register must be aged 16 or over and must be resident in the United Kingdom for a minimum period, which is intended to be 3 months. Although both the age limit and the qualifying period of residence could be varied by Regulations. Foreign tourists coming here for less than 3 months would not need to register, but could use the passport or identity card on which they entered the United Kingdom as proof of their identity. Most people will be entered on the Register because they apply for one of the "family" of identity cards. However, the Register will be more than just a database of people holding identity cards. Entries will be held on people who make an application for an identity card whether or not that application is granted and the Register will also be able to hold information if it is available about people who have not applied for an identity card (e.g. illegal entrants) as well as people who are no longer resident in the United Kingdom.

2.12 **Comments are invited on the proposals for a National Identity Register as set out in Clauses 1-3 of the draft Bill.**

Issue of ID cards and designation of existing documents as ID cards

2.13 The draft Bill at Clause 8(1) provides that an ID card may be a card which is issued to an individual by the Secretary of State (these are what have been described as "plain" cards) **or** a card which forms part of or is issued with a "designated document" and which shows, records or stores identity information.

2.14 The term "ID card" used in the draft Bill therefore covers any card that may be designated as one of the "family" of identity cards including a plain identity card.

2.15 The process of designation means that it is not necessary to specify on the face of the bill exactly which cards will become ID cards. It also will be possible to phase in the scheme by designating different categories of card at different times to be issued by designated documents authorities as set out at Clause 10. This is consistent with the Government's intention to adopt an incremental approach to the introduction of identity cards.

2.16 The "family" of compatible identification cards could include: -

- a passport identity card (valid for travel and issued to British citizens);
- a driving licence photocard;
- a residence permit card for foreign nationals;
- a special residence permit (or "registration certificate") card for European Economic Area (EEA) nationals;
- a "plain" identity card available for those who do not qualify for or do not wish to have one of the other cards.

2.17 It is intended that most people will obtain a card when they first obtain or renew either their driving licence or their passport, and their new document will double as an ID card. If they hold both a passport and a driving licence they will be able to use both documents as an ID card. Once a document such as a passport has been designated as an ID card, this will be the only form in which it will be available – i.e. there will be no "non-ID card" variants. It would undermine confidence in the system if there were to be identity documents available, on demand, at different levels of security. Nevertheless, the process for issuing the ID card versions of designated documents will take full account of applicants' individual circumstances. Thus it could be decided to make less rigorous checks on certain applicants (for example the very elderly), but that would be within the scope of the identity cards scheme.

2.18 For those that do not qualify for or wish to obtain an ID card as part of a designated document, stand-alone 'plain' ID cards would be available. For foreign residents – including European Economic Area nationals – the card is likely to take the form of a residence permit card.

2.19 When applying for an ID card, it will be necessary to make a personal application so that a biometric can be recorded. This is likely to be at a convenient local or regional centre – this could be either an existing public office or at a newly created enrolment centre. Applicants will be asked to bring along existing identity documentation, which will be checked for authenticity and validity. A digital photograph will be taken and biometric information such as finger scans and/or iris images will be recorded. It will be within the scope of the identity cards scheme to have special arrangements to make enrolment checks less rigorous on certain applicants (for example the very elderly).

2.20 The precise arrangements for making an application for an ID card as well as the design of the cards themselves will be decided as the identity cards programme progresses following further preparatory work and testing of different options. These arrangements are therefore not spelt out on the face of the draft bill. Rather provision is included for the detailed arrangements to be set out in Regulations. Clause 5(3) of the draft bill makes clear that an application for registration and thus issue of an ID card must be accompanied by information to be prescribed and Clause 5(4) enables further information to be required in order to verify the information the applicant has already provided.

2.21 Clause 8(8) allows the format of an ID card and the way in which information is to be recorded on it to be specified in Regulations, but these would be subject to the affirmative resolution procedure and so would need to be approved formally by both Houses of

Parliament. Agreeing the format of the cards is best left to regulations so that this can be set nearer to the time of the introduction of the cards scheme. Regulations can also be amended to provide necessary improvements and to ensure that there is linkage with the format of documents designated as ID cards as these may already be determined by EU or international standards. Fees for ID cards will also be established by Regulations made under Clause 37 of the draft Bill.

2.22 Clause 12 of the draft Bill provides a power to make Regulations concerning how changes which might affect the accuracy of the Register must be notified. This will be used to require people who are registered to notify important changes, such as changes to their name, address or nationality. Clause 12(6) makes anyone who fails to follow such a requirement liable to a civil penalty not exceeding £1000. This is a lesser penalty than applies currently to holders of driving licences, who may be liable to criminal proceedings for failure to notify changes of address etc. However, the more serious criminal sanction for driving licences is justified as it is particularly important, in order to enforce road traffic law and to trace drivers involved in accidents, that the police are able to rely on the Driver and Vehicle Licensing Agency and Driver and Vehicle Licensing Northern Ireland to have up-to-date information on the addresses of drivers.

2.23 **Comments are invited on the proposals for the issue of ID cards and designation of existing documents as ID cards as set out in Clauses 4-5, 8 – 10, 12 and 37 of the draft Bill.**

Data sharing powers

2.24 The "Identity Cards: the Next Steps" document made clear that applications for one of the family of identity cards will require checks to be made against other databases. This would be in addition to enabling the National Identity Register to confirm, with an individual's consent, the identity information provided by an organisation wishing to verify the identity of a person who has produced an identity card.

2.25 Data sharing would help establish that an application for a card is genuine. The data-sharing gateways established for this purpose will be used only when processing applications for cards or related purposes (e.g. when issuing a replacement) to ensure that the person, who applies to register and to be issued with an identity card, is the person he or she claims to be. They do not confer any general power to share data for wider purposes than set out in the draft Bill.

2.26 The Cabinet Office study on Identity Fraud (published in July 2002) recommended that existing procedures for issuing driving licences and passports should be strengthened and recommended greater use of biographical checks on applicants. These checks could, for example, confirm that a person had been known by a certain identity and lived at known addresses for a number of years. This information will be much more difficult for a fraudster to know, to change, or to fabricate and will guard against completely bogus identities. It will also add an additional layer of checking rather than relying simply on documents which can be stolen or forged.

2.27 The most effective way of confirming this biographical information is to check some of the information provided by applicants with information held on a range of Government and private sector databases. Most people will be familiar with checks being made against other databases, with their consent, when they apply for financial services such as insurance or credit cards.

2.28 However, in the case of an application for an identity card there will be no question of withholding consent to such checks. The draft Bill provides therefore at Clause 11 data-sharing gateways to allow, and to place a duty on, controllers of other databases to provide information needed to verify an individual's application.

2.29 The databases that could be checked would include public sector bodies (such as the National Insurance or DVLA databases) as well as private sector organisations (such as credit reference agencies or banks). Information requested would be restricted to that needed to confirm the identity of an individual who has made an application to register. Confidential information relating to the particular service and not relevant to checking identity would not be accessible. Thus the National Identity Register would be able to seek confirmation of names, dates of birth or addresses but not information that was not needed to confirm identity such as the level of National Insurance contributions paid by an individual. Particular data sharing gateways can therefore only be established with the consent of Parliament and for the limited purpose of validating information on the Register.

2.30 The Secretary of State (or a body appointed on his behalf) would hold and administer the National Identity Register and be responsible for ensuring that any data sharing was carried out in accordance with the law. In order to allow for testing of the identity cards scheme in advance of the first cards being issued, these data sharing powers could be piloted or tested in advance of the identity cards scheme.

2.31   As a clear statement of the importance with which the Government views the integrity of the National Identity Register, it has been decided to introduce at Clause 29 (1) a specific criminal offence if anyone involved in the operation of the Register or the identity cards system discloses any information without lawful authority.

2.32   **Comments are invited on the proposals for data sharing of information that needs to be checked in order to issue identity cards as set out in Clause 11 of the draft Bill.**

Disclosure of National Identity Register information

2.33   There will be an exception to the general bar on disclosing information from the Register where disclosure is in the interests of national security and for the prevention and investigation of crime. The disclosure of information to the police and security and intelligence agencies will be allowed only for specified purposes and subject to a an internal authorisation and independent oversight.

2.34   There will be a general power under Clause 20 to disclose information about an individual held on the Register to the **security and intelligence agencies** for their purposes, e.g. as on the grounds of national security.

2.35   **Law enforcement agencies** including Customs and Excise and the Inland Revenue will be able to seek disclosure of information from the Register for specified purposes e.g. for the prevention or investigation of crime. This will also apply to the Immigration Service which, as a part of the Secretary of State's department, does not need to be named on the face of the Bill. Disclosure will also be allowed in prescribed cases to other Secretaries of State such as the Department for Work and Pensions for example to help investigate benefit fraud. For these groups, disclosure of "audit trails" of card usage is permitted only in cases of serious crime. The definition of serious crime is based on that used in the Regulation of Investigatory Powers Act 2000 and requires that: -

a)   it involves the use of violence, results in substantial financial gain or is conducted by a large number of persons in pursuit of a common purpose, or

b)   the offence or one of the offences is an offence for which a person who has attained the age of twenty-one and has no previous convictions could reasonably be expected to be sentenced to imprisonment for a term of three years or more.

2.36   In addition under Clause 24(1) the Police and Immigration Service will have a power to check a person's biometric against the National Identity Register if it has not been possible to identify them otherwise. This could also include a check of a fingerprint found at the scene of a crime against the Register should it be technically feasible to do so and where checks against police fingerprint databases have proved fruitless.

2.37   There will have to be appropriate authorisation of any requests for disclosure from the Register and the draft Bill allows for different procedures to apply depending on the sensitivity of the information being disclosed. In addition Clause 22 provides a power of disclosure for the purpose of correcting false information (e.g. on another government database).

2.38   The draft Bill provides at Clauses 25 and 26 for oversight of the procedures for disclosing personal information from the National Identity Register. This would be by establishing a "National Identity Scheme Commissioner". For clarity the draft Bill provides for a new person to undertake these functions though in practice they might be carried out by inviting existing bodies to undertake them.

2.39   **Comments are invited on the proposals for disclosure of information from the National Identity Register without consent for purposes such as the prevention and investigation of crime and on grounds of national security as set out in Clauses 20-24 of the draft Bill and also on the options for oversight in Clauses 25 and 26.**

Criminal offences and other sanctions

2.40   Clauses 27-32 of the draft Bill establish new offences relating to the identity cards scheme as well as wider offences relating to "identity documents" more generally.

2.41   Clause 27 establishes two levels of seriousness of offences of possession of a false identity document. The more serious (at Clause 27 (1) and (2)) is where it can be shown that a person knows or believes that the document they hold is false or was improperly obtained, or relates to someone else, or they have machinery or apparatus for making false identity documents. These offences would be liable to a maximum term of 10 years imprisonment.

2.42   The lesser offence at Clause 27(3) is where it can not be proven that the person was aware of the nature of their false document. This would make it an offence without reasonable excuse to have a false or improperly obtained document, or one that relates to someone else, with a maximum penalty of 2 years imprisonment.

2.43   Clause 29 makes it an offence for any person to disclose information from the Register without lawful authority. Clause 30 makes it an offence to provide false information when making an application to be entered on the Register or providing information to secure another person's application. This offence has a maximum penalty of 2 years imprisonment. Clause 31 extends the Computer Misuse Act of 1990 to make it an offence, with a maximum penalty of 10 years imprisonment, to tamper with the National Identity Register, including creating a false or bogus entry on the Register.

2.44   Clauses 33-36 of the draft Bill set out the procedures for civil penalties that may be applied for example for failing to notify changes affecting the accuracy of the Register under Clause 12 or failure to register when required to do so once Clause 6 of the Bill is brought into effect. It also sets out the procedures for giving notice of a civil penalty and for resolving disputes and dealing with appeals against the imposition of a civil penalty.

2.45   **Comments are invited on the proposals for criminal offences and civil penalties relating to identity cards as set out in Clauses 27-36 of the draft Bill.**

Identity fraud

2.46   In July 2002 the Cabinet Office published "Identity Fraud: A Study". Identity fraud has been recognised as an important and growing problem which costs the UK economy an estimated £1.3bn per annum. The study complemented the consultation carried out by the Home Office on entitlement cards. One of the study's conclusions was that the creation of a single document could be beneficial in replacing the present 'mosaic' of documents used to establish identity if accompanied by much more secure processes for the issue and use of the document.

2.47   Alongside the work on identity cards, the Home Office is leading on work with both public and private sector organisations to implement measures against identity fraud that can be put in place in advance of an identity cards scheme. Examples of early progress on this include aligning the penalties for making fraudulent applications for passports and driving licences in the Criminal Justice Act 2003 and setting up, in December 2003, a UK Passport Service database of lost and stolen passports.

2.48   The criminal offences in Clauses 27 and 28 of the draft Bill have been drafted to provide that new offences should not apply just to ID cards issued under the draft Identity Cards Bill but also will apply to other identity documents. These include UK passports, immigration documents and driving licences whether or not they have been yet designated as ID cards. It also covers driving licences, passports or identity cards issued by other countries.

2.49   It is intended that these provisions should be brought into force as soon as practicable after the Identity Cards Bill receives Royal Assent in order to provide an immediate and stronger deterrent to the possession of any false or improperly obtained identity documents.

2.50   **Comments are invited on the proposals for criminal offences relating to wider identity fraud as set out in Clauses 27-28 of the draft Bill.**

Compulsion

2.51   The Government has made clear that it is planning to build the base for a **compulsory** national identity cards scheme, but that this will be in two stages. The first will be linked to the designation of existing documents (such as passport or driving licence photocards) as ID cards. The second would involve a move to compulsion once the initial stage has been rolled out to a significant coverage of the population and the Government is satisfied that the conditions set out in Identity Cards: the Next Steps were met.

2.52   The draft Bill provides for the second, compulsory, stage of the identity cards scheme at Clause 6 by establishing a power to make it a requirement to register. This power would enable a date to be set at which point it would become an obligation to register. However, **this will only be brought into force at a later date once the initial stage of the identity cards scheme has been successfully completed and following a debate and Vote in both Houses of Parliament**. Regulations made under this clause would be subject to the affirmative resolution procedure but, in addition, the draft Bill provides at Clause 7 that the Government could not table these Regulations until it has published a full report that has been approved by both Houses of Parliament. The Government's report would set out its case for the move to compulsion and cover all relevant aspects of the proposal. This report would be laid before Parliament to allow for a period of consideration before both Houses were invited to debate and approve (with the possibility of amendment) the Government's proposition in the report.

2.53   Once introduced the requirement would be to register and thus to provide the information necessary for the issue of an identity card. **There will not be a requirement to carry an identity card** and once registered there will be no **automatic** obligation to use the card that has been issued e.g. to access public or private services where evidence of identity is needed. However, once it has been made a requirement to register, it will be possible for individual services to establish their own procedures which could include making Regulations requiring that an identity card must be produced to establish the identity of an applicant for that service.

2.54   Not only would the requirement to register be brought into force at a later date, but it will be possible for it to be phased in by specifying which groups of individuals will be required to register and setting a date in the future by which this must be completed. This means that it would be possible, for example, to require all people within a particular age band to register and to set a clear timetable for doing so.

2.55   Once the requirement to register is in place it would not become a criminal offence to fail to register and there would be no question of individuals being fined by the courts or imprisoned as a result of a failure to register.

2.56   The draft Bill provides that a civil financial penalty, as distinct from a fine, may be applied of up to £2,500 if someone fails to register when required to do so. Such penalties would not be automatic and it would therefore be possible to exercise discretion as to when any penalty should be applied and also what action to take to recover any penalty if it is not paid. Any debts incurred as a result of unpaid penalties could be enforced through the civil courts.

2.57   Experience suggests that in other countries with compulsory card schemes it is more likely to be the inconvenience of not having a card that encourages people to obtain one, rather than any theoretical risk of a penalty.

2.58   **Comments are invited on the power to set a date when it would become a compulsory requirement to register as set out in Clauses 6 and 7 of the draft Bill.**

Requirements to use identity cards

2.59   The identity card scheme will immediately provide a more convenient way for people to show their identity when accessing public or private sector services if they choose to do so and where the service wishes to check their identity. Until it becomes compulsory to register the identity card would not be the only way of proving identity. In the "Next Steps" paper it was made clear that it would not be **mandatory** to use an identity card to help verify entitlement to services during the first stage of the scheme, in effect before it was compulsory to register for a card. The draft Bill makes this prohibition clear.

2.60   Following a move to the second stage of the scheme when it would be a requirement to register and obtain a card it would be possible to make Regulations that would make use of the card compulsory to access certain public services. This would further help prevent unauthorised and fraudulent access to those services. However, when the scheme becomes compulsory there would be no automatic requirement for an identity card to be produced to access public services. There would need to be a separate decision for each service.

2.61   In addition the draft Bill includes at Clauses 15-19 an order making power which would provide by Regulations when an identity card may be required to access a particular service. However, it would be used only in cases where it was clear that that there are no or insufficient powers already in place to make Regulations for a particular service or circumstance.

2.62   There are further limits on how this power can be used, for example it will not be possible to use the power to make it compulsory to carry a card. Also in making Regulations under this power, the Government would have to explain why existing powers to make Regulations about that service were inadequate. Regulations under this power would be made by affirmative order and published in draft for consultation prior to being laid.

2.63   The draft Bill would not automatically require the production of a card for any service. Parliament would have to agree revised Regulations for each service. Regulations made under this new power would be laid by the responsible Secretary of State and so the Government and Parliament would always be in control of the rules for how the card scheme would be used by public services.

2.64   It is not intended to inhibit voluntary use of the card in either the public or private sector. Some businesses already insist on production of "photo-ID", while others adopt a 'menu' approach, allowing clients to confirm their identity through production of a range of documents. Industry will continue to be free to decide what measures they put in place to counter the risk they face of identity fraud. However, in the first stage of the scheme an identity card would not be the only document that could be required as proof of identity and Clause 19 will make it unlawful for anyone to require the production of an identity card unless they also allow a reasonable alternative method of establishing identity to be equally acceptable. This would be enforceable in civil proceedings but in consulting on this provision, the Government would like views on whether other ways of enforcing this sanction would be more acceptable.

2.65   In addition, it is intended to establish an accreditation scheme so that only those private sector organisations that have been approved (which might include banks, building societies or airlines) would be able to make checks on the National Identity Register on the validity of cards or the registered details. Accreditation would be removed if a particular business attempted to misuse the service.

2.66   Verification of identity will be done by matching an individual cardholder with one or more of the components of the system:

- The data printed on the face of the identity card;
- The data stored on the identity card's chip;
- The data stored on the National Identity Register.

2.67   The Scheme will be flexible in offering different levels of card check to suit the particular transactions and the needs of accredited card checkers. For example:

- retailers or licensees wanting to check proof of age might just check the person against the photograph on the card and the date of birth;
- banks or building societies might check a person's biometric (using a card reader) and verify this against the National Identity Register before opening an account;
- employers might confirm a cardholder's immigration status by way of an automated telephone check of the National Identity Register.

2.68   Public and private sector organisations' verification checks of cards will **not** give access to the contents of the database or the details of the biometric. They will simply confirm identity and other relevant details (e.g. immigration status to show that the cardholder could be employed lawfully). An online verification of the holder's biometric would confirm that the person presenting the card was the person to whom it had been issued in a similar way that a retailer can seek online authorisation of a transaction with a credit or debit card without being told what is the cardholder's credit limit or bank balance.

2.69   We anticipate that over the period when the identity cards scheme is being introduced and the National Identity Register established, developments in technology will make sophisticated card readers more readily available. Banks and other financial institutions, as well as the retail sector, increasingly make use of such technology to read smart cards. The Home Office is engaged in discussions with stakeholders about the way in which card readers could best be deployed. Discussions will continue with Department of Work and Pensions, the DTI, as well as the Local Government Association and organisations including the CBI and the TUC.

2.70   The National Identity Register will hold individuals' confirmed identity information securely and an audit of checks made of entries on the Register (whether or not via an ID card) will be held on the database. Disclosure of the details of a person's audit log records will not be possible without his or her consent other than to law enforcement agencies and the security and intelligence services when investigating serious crime and matters of national security. There will be strict controls and independent oversight of these arrangements.

2.71   **Comments are invited on the power as set out in Clauses 15-19 of the draft Bill to make Regulations on the use of a card, where existing powers relating to the service concerned are not adequate, including views on the provision described in paragraph 2.64 and how it may be enforced.**

Devolution

2.72   The identity cards scheme is intended primarily as a United Kingdom wide measure to help deter and control illegal immigration by helping to establish the nationality and immigration status of UK residents which is why the "registrable facts" which need to be held in the Register include nationality and immigration status. Immigration and nationality are matters specifically reserved in the Scotland Act 1998 (Schedule 5 Part II B6) and have not been devolved in relation to Wales or Northern Ireland. This includes British citizenship, the status of people in the United Kingdom who are not British citizens, free movement within the European Union and European Economic Area (EEA) and the issue of passports or other travel documents.

2.73   The identity cards scheme will be a United Kingdom wide scheme. This will be in exactly the same way as the issue of British passports and residence documents for EEA and foreign nationals resident in the UK is a UK Government responsibility carried out by the Home Office. Accordingly, the registration of individuals on the National Identity Register and the issue to them of identity cards will be matters reserved to the United Kingdom government irrespective of whether a person resides in England, Scotland, Wales or Northern Ireland.

2.74   This would also include the second stage of the scheme when it would become compulsory to register and be issued with an identity card. There will, however, be a number of practical issues, which have been the subject of ongoing discussions with the devolved administrations. For example, the issue of driving licences is reserved in the Scotland Act, (Schedule 5 Part II E1) but is operated separately in Northern Ireland. The intention is that the substantive legislation should allow the driving licence in both Great Britain and in

Northern Ireland to serve as one of the "family" of identity cards but bringing the Northern Ireland driving licence into the scheme would require discussion with any devolved administration in Northern Ireland.

2.75   Criminal offences relating to documents or a database that operate on a UK-wide basis, i.e. identity cards and the National Identity Register, apply throughout the UK including in Scotland.

2.76   However, there are some exceptions in the draft Bill where territorial extent varies. The order making power in Clause 15(1) enables Departments to make regulations linking production of an identity card with access to its services where such a power does not currently exist. This clause does not extend to Scotland. Clause 1(3) of the draft Bill makes clear that any use of the Register and card scheme is not authorised in Scotland for devolved matters (as opposed to the establishment of the Register and the issuing of cards). The Scottish Parliament would have to pass its own enabling legislation if the Register and card scheme were ever to be used in Scotland for devolved purposes. Similarly a requirement to use an identity card to access public services that have been devolved in Wales or Northern Ireland would be a matter for the National Assembly for Wales or for any devolved authority in Northern Ireland as appropriate. However in these cases the enabling powers to make such measures are included in the draft Bill as the devolution arrangements for Wales and Northern Ireland are different from Scotland.

2.77   There is also a power in the draft Bill to disclose information on the National Identity Register to law enforcement agencies. For Scottish agencies this would be only for reserved matters, for example investigating terrorist crimes. Examples where the police would have powers in the rest of the UK but not in Scotland would be when investigating common law crimes unrelated to reserved matters, such as criminal offences in Scotland of murder or other crimes of violence.

2.78   **Comments are invited on the proposals on the application of the draft Identity Cards Bill and the use of identity cards in Scotland, Wales and Northern Ireland.**

Chapter 3

WIDER ISSUES NOT INCLUDED IN THE DRAFT LEGISLATION

Programme management

3.1　The Government is determined to ensure that the Programme to develop a national identity cards scheme is managed to the highest standards, and that the major business change and information technology challenges are dealt with effectively. An interdepartmental **Identity Cards Programme Board** has, therefore, been set up, under the chairmanship of the Home Office, to co-ordinate and drive forward the Government's proposals for the development of a national identity cards scheme.

3.2　The Board is chaired by John Gieve, Permanent Secretary at the Home Office, and includes the Home Office senior responsible owner, Helen Edwards, together with senior representatives of the main Departments and Agencies involved in the delivery of the Identity Cards Programme. These include the Department for Transport, Department for Work and Pensions, Office of the Deputy Prime Minister, Foreign and Commonwealth Office, Inland Revenue, Office for National Statistics, UK Passport Service and Home Office Immigration and Nationality Directorate.

3.3　The Identity Cards Programme will be subject to continuing external review by the Office for Government Commerce (OGC) Gateway process. The key phases of the programme are: -

- a **programme definition** phase, focusing on the design of the scheme, feasibility, procurement requirements and legislation, running from early 2004 to 2005;
- a **procurement phase**, focusing on procuring the delivery partners who will implement the scheme, starting in 2005, and ending on the signing of contracts with delivery partners in 2006;
- an **implementation phase**, from 2006 to 2007;
- a volume end-to-end **testing phase**, from 2007;
- on current plans leading to the **first cards being issued** towards the end of 2007-08.

LEGISLATION ON IDENTITY CARDS

Governance and the issuing process

3.4　Decisions on **governance** for the identity cards issuing process are important but will not require any specific legislation unless it is decided to establish a separate organisation in statute (for example a non-departmental public body) to be responsible for the identity cards scheme. It is proposed that after the consultation on draft legislation the Government should decide whether a good case has been made for having any type of arms length governance structure and, if so, whether it would require legislation. Accordingly, **the Government invites comments on the options for a governance structure for the identity cards scheme**.

3.5　There are a number of possible governance options, including maintaining the scheme within a central Department such as the Home Office, an Executive Agency, a non-Departmental Public Body or a non-Ministerial Department. Only some of these options require any specific legislation.

3.6　How the scheme will be governed is a key question for the Identity Cards Programme Board. The governing authority is likely to have such functions as:

- oversight of the scheme;
- setting the standards for enrolment and card issuing;
- regulation to ensure consistency between different cards designated as identity cards;
- establishing security specifications for documents and systems;
- owning and having accountability for the information on the National Identity Register; and
- authorising disclosure of information held on the Register, for example to the police investigating serious crimes.

3.7　We have not closed off any options nor decided finally whether there should be a governance structure established in legislation. However, the Government's preferred option at this stage is an Executive Agency with its powers delegated from the Home Secretary. This could be an existing agency and would **not** require legislation. There are therefore no clauses on governance in the draft Bill.

32

3.8   The preferred option of an executive agency was reached after considering the following criteria: -

- maintaining standards for identity cards – an ability to set clear rules in order to maintain the required technology, security and service levels;
- public confidence – clear lines of accountability through Ministers to the public and Parliament;
- enforcement mechanisms – an ability to direct those involved in any part of the card issuing process to comply with standards; and
- financial implications – ability to set, charge and account for fees.

3.9   Decisions on the type of governing authority are separate from decisions as to the organisational structure and whether one or a number of different agencies will be involved in the processes for issuing identity cards. Many of the processes (e.g. card manufacture) may be contracted out to the private sector, as they have been for passports, but no decisions have yet been taken. The process for issuing identity cards will involve a number of separate functions such as:

- identity enrolment;
- identity maintenance;
- identity verification;
- card manufacturing; and
- processing payments.

3.10   Decisions on who will undertake these functions and whether some processes will continue to be carried out by existing agencies have yet to be taken.

3.11   **Views are invited on options for the governance arrangements for the scheme.**

Police powers

3.12   There will be no change to police powers relating to stop and search and the Government has made clear that it will not be a requirement to carry an identity card or to produce a card to a police officer on demand.

3.13   However, the introduction of identity cards will make it much easier and simpler for people to prove their identity when they wish to do so. ID cards will therefore be useful for the police and for law-abiding citizens. Existing police powers to require drivers to produce their driving licence (which could be designated as an ID card) on demand or within 7 days at a police station will remain. Also if someone has been arrested for a recordable offence existing powers will allow the police to take reasonable steps to identify them. This currently includes powers to take fingerprints. If it were not possible to identify an arrested person otherwise, it is intended that a check could be made on the person's biometric against the National Identity Register.

3.14   As at present with existing documents, people will be free to produce an identity card on a voluntary basis (if they have one) to a police officer or to any other official as a means of establishing their identity and for it to be confirmed that their card is genuine. Many people will find no problem with this and indeed will find it useful to be able to identify themselves reliably in this way. The intention is that people will be able to have their biometrics checked against the Register even in the absence of a card on a voluntary basis in order to be able to demonstrate their identity if, for example, they are stopped by the police.

Costs, fee levels and technical specification

3.15   The draft Identity Cards Bill does **not** lay down the detailed specification for identity cards or the detailed arrangements for making applications. These will be set out later in Regulations.

3.16   The Government's intention is that cards would be issued free to 16 year olds, and reduced-fee cards would be available to those on low incomes. Everyone else will pay a standard charge. The charge will be either an increase on the fee for a designated document (such as a passport or driving licence) or just a straight fee for the plain identity card. People who have both a passport and a driving licence would only pay the uplift once (i.e. it would not apply to both documents). Building on existing systems will give more opportunities for keeping additional costs down as some of the activities needed for the identity cards scheme are already carried out by agencies like DVLA and the UK Passport Service as part of their current procedures.

3.17   Most people will join the scheme when they apply for or renew their driving licence or passport for which charges are already levied. The minimum charge to obtain a 10-year passport from the UK Passport Service is £42 and the full cost of obtaining an initial 10-year driving licence from DVLA is £38. In practice the cost that many people currently pay for these documents is around £8-£10 higher when taking account of the cost of photographs and services that check that forms have been completed correctly and the right documentation enclosed. These costs would be included in a national identity cards scheme.

3.18   If the Government did not implement a scheme which covered everyone but concentrated purely on implementing more secure passports and driving licences including biometrics, initial estimates suggest that the 10 year cost of passports would rise to around £73 and driving licences to around £69. Under the national identity cards scheme, our best initial estimates are that: -

- a 10 year plain identity card would cost most people in the order of £35;
- a combined passport/identity card would cost £77; and
- a combined driving licence/identity card would cost £73 (though holders of both a driving licence and a passport would only pay the full cost for the first one they renewed).

In other words the estimated additional cost for holders of passports or driving licences would be around £4 per person spread across 10 years.

Citizen Information Project

3.19   Alongside work on identity cards the government is considering options for developing a population register to include the whole UK population. This exercise, the **Citizen Information Project** (CIP), is a cross-cutting government initiative designed to support more efficient, responsive and personalised public services. Such a population register would contain basic contact information for everyone in the UK drawn from existing administrative records. Preliminary studies indicate that its creation could lead to significant cost and efficiency savings in delivering public services and improvements in the quality of those services. There are also substantial potential statistical benefits in such a system that would benefit the development of and evaluation of evidence-based policy making. On 6 January 2004 the Registrar General published a summary of the findings of a feasibility study on the Citizen Information Project - for further information go to:
http://www.statistics.gov.uk/registration/cip.asp

3.20   The Government also announced that it had commissioned further detailed development work to be carried out over the next 18 months by a team based within the General Register Office – part of the Office for National Statistics (ONS). This further stage will include work on the draft legislation needed to establish a population register and create the conditions to allow it to operate. In addition to setting out the role of the body charged with operating the population register, the legislation would also introduce concrete safeguards for the public concerning the use of these data to be enshrined in law that is compliant with data protection and privacy laws. This stage will also include public consultation to explore the issues around public acceptability of the proposal.

3.21   The National Identity Register and a population register are separate but complementary proposals, and they serve different purposes. The identity cards initiative and the CIP are working closely together to ensure coherence and to eliminate unnecessary duplication including costs. Although the successful implementation of a population register should enable the issuing of identity cards to be streamlined, making it quicker and easier to establish eligibility, its main aim is to improve the delivery of wider government services. Where the population register becomes aware of a change in individual circumstances that has been recorded by other government databases in the course of day to day service delivery, this information would be able to flow across Government to help ensure that other services continue to be directed towards to the correct person. These issues will be explored in the next stage of development of a population register, and be part of its legal framework. The Government is open to the possibility of including provisions relating to the creation and operation of a separate population register within the identity cards legislation but this depends on the progress of CIP development work when the Identity Cards Bill is introduced.

Biometrics

3.22   There will be close work across Government to develop effective technology for the identity cards programme, and especially for biometrics. A biometric is a unique identifying physical characteristic. Examples include facial recognition, iris patterns and fingerprints. There is close co-operation between projects to include biometrics on identity cards and passports and immigration developments including Application Registration Cards issued to asylum seekers.

3.23   The UK Passport Service has been supporting the work of the International Civil Aviation Organisation (ICAO) to develop international standards for biometric deployment. ICAO nominated facial recognition as the primary biometric for travel documents with fingerprint (and possibly iris pattern) as secondary but not mandatory. In line with ICAO recommendations, a biometric British passport is to be introduced that will deploy contactless integrated circuit media (i.e. a computer chip) to store a facial image biometric. A contactless chip includes an aerial to allow close proximity readings, i.e. without being swiped through a reader. Modern contactless chips are paper-thin and therefore particularly suited to being incorporated in passport books or passport identity cards.

3.24   The Home Secretary also announced on 11 November 2003 that the UK Passport Service (in collaboration with DVLA, the Immigration and Nationality Directorate, and the Home Office Identity Cards Programme) will be running a **biometric enrolment trial**. The trial will evaluate issues around biometric recording using facial recognition, iris pattern and fingerprint. Over six months it will enrol 10,000 volunteers using several locations (including mobile units) to ensure a representative coverage of the population.

3.25   Personal attendance to enrol the biometric will be necessary for each identity card applicant. Recording biometric information will take place at local and regional, convenient access points and will help to ensure that an identity record is associated with information unique to that person. The biometric information can be stored securely on a chip on the card as well as on the National Identity Register. The uniqueness of biometric information will help prevent people's identities being stolen and also will confirm securely a person's identity when a card is checked and deter fraudsters from attempting to register more than one identity.

International developments

3.26   We cannot stay aloof from a range of wider developments internationally. International travel has increased dramatically over the past 50 years. Nearly 90 million passengers arrive each year at United Kingdom ports and, although most of these are returning residents or genuine visitors, the task of controlling immigration is becoming much harder.

3.27   Terrorist atrocities in the United States on 11 September 2001 and elsewhere have shown a pressing need to improve the security of international travel on top of existing controls on immigration. This has included the use of biometrics as a way of identifying individuals more securely. The United States has introduced a biometric system known as "**US VISIT**" for visitors arriving from abroad. It requires finger scan biometrics as well as a digital photograph and is used to verify an individual's identity, link their entry to previous visits as well as providing a way of checking people in and out of the country reliably.

3.28   The European Union has recently considered Regulations on common standards for **biometric security features to be included in common format visas and residence permits** for foreign, i.e. non-EU, nationals. Agreement has now been reached on these measures but (at the time of publication) they have yet to be adopted formally. However, the special European Council held following the Madrid bombings has given added emphasis to the need to improve the security of travel documents.

3.29   Since January 2002, the Immigration and Nationality Directorate of the Home Office has been issuing **Application Registration Cards** to asylum seekers and their dependants. These cards incorporate photographs and fingerprint biometrics. In addition since July 2003 fingerprints and photographs have been taken from all visa applicants for United Kingdom visas at our visa issuing post in Sri Lanka and this is being extended to visa applicants in East Africa.

3.30   As well as the benefits the identity cards scheme will bring, our active plans for biometric identity cards will ensure that the United Kingdom can exercise real influence in the international debates on standards. Taken together, all these factors make the time right now for the United Kingdom to develop its own identity cards scheme incorporating biometric technology.

Chapter 4

Conclusion and summary of consultation points

Summary of consultation points

4.1   There are a number of specific consultation points that we have highlighted in this paper and these are summarised here for convenience. The specific consultation points are on:

1) proposals for a National Identity Register as set out in Clauses 1-3 of the draft Bill (paragraph 2.12);

2) proposals for the issue of ID cards and designation of existing documents as ID cards as set out in Clauses 4, 5, 8-10, 12 and 37 of the draft Bill (paragraph 2.23);

3) data sharing of information that needs to be checked in order to issue identity cards as set out in Clause 11 of the draft Bill (paragraph 2.32);

4) disclosure of information from the National Identity Register without consent for the prevention and investigation of crime and on grounds of national security as set out in Clauses 20-24 of the draft Bill and also on the options for oversight in clauses 25-26 (paragraph 2.39);

5) criminal offences and civil penalties relating to identity cards as set out in Clauses 27-36 of the draft Bill (paragraph 2.45);

6) wider identity fraud issues as set out in Clauses 27-28 of the draft Bill (paragraph 2.50);

7) the power to set a date when it would become a compulsory requirement to register as set out in Clauses 6-7 of the draft Bill (paragraph 2.58);

8) the power as set out in Clauses 15-19 of the draft Bill to make Regulations on the use of a card, where existing powers relating to the service concerned are not adequate, including views on the provision described in paragraph 2.64 and how it may be enforced (paragraph 2.71);

9) proposals on the application of the draft Identity Cards Bill and the use of identity cards in Scotland, Wales and Northern Ireland (paragraph 2.78);

10) options for a governance structure for the identity cards scheme (paragraph 3.11).

4.2   In addition the Government invites **any** wider comments on its legislative proposals for identity cards.

4.3   The purpose of this consultation is to help the Government to introduce the legislation that will enable the identity cards scheme to be introduced in the most effective way. The draft Bill has been drafted on the basis that all the practical issues outstanding will be resolved as part of the identity cards programme and that the Government will reserve until later any final decision on the timing of a move to compulsion.

Next steps

4.4   The Government will take account of **all** comments on the draft Identity Cards legislation including any recommendations from the Home Affairs Committee.

4.5   Once the Government has taken stock of these comments following this consultation, it intends introducing a substantive Bill on identity cards as soon as Parliamentary time allows. This would be based on the draft Bill at **Annex A** to this paper, but with any changes or additions needed to take account of this consultation as well as any further developments of the identity cards programme.

Consultation criteria

4.6   This consultation is being carried out in line with the Government's six consultation criteria. These are that we will:

1)   Consult widely throughout the process, allowing a minimum of 12 weeks for written consultation;
2)   Be clear about what the proposals are, who may be affected, what questions are being asked and the timescale for responses;
3)   Ensure that the consultation is clear, concise and widely accessible;
4)   Give feedback regarding the responses received and how the consultation process influenced the policy;
5)   Monitor the department's effectiveness at consultation (including through the use of a designated consultation co-ordinator);
6)   Ensure the consultation follows better regulation best practice.

4.7   If you have any complaints or comments about the consultation process, you should contact the Home Office consultation co-ordinator:

Pio Smith
Consultation Co-ordinator
Performance and Delivery Unit
Better Government Team
9th Floor, South
Home Office
50 Queen Anne's Gate
London SW1H 9AT

pio.smith31@homeoffice.gsi.gov.uk

How to submit comments and closing date

4.8   Copies of this consultation paper and previous documents on identity cards are available on the **identity cards website** at: www.identitycards.gov.uk

4.9   Comments are invited on both the general scope of the legislation proposed as well as any detailed drafting points on the clauses of the draft Identity Cards Bill.

4.10   All comments received on the consultation paper may be published unless the person or organisation making them asks specifically that they should **not** be published. We will assume that you are content for us to do this if you are replying by e-mail, irrespective of any standard confidentiality disclaimer generated by your IT system, unless you include a specific request for confidentiality in the main text of your submission. Responses to the consultation may (subject to any requests for confidentiality) be passed on to the Home Affairs Committee in the context of their pre-legislative scrutiny of the draft Bill. Anyone wishing their comments to be taken into account by the Committee should be aware that they are working to a much tighter timetable so that they can submit their considered views as part of this consultation. The Committee will also issue its own invitation to submit written evidence on the draft Bill. Responses relating to Scotland, Wales and Northern Ireland may also be passed to the devolved administrations, subject again to any requests for confidentiality.

4.11   Any comments should be sent to:

Robin Woodland
Legislation Consultation
Identity Cards Programme
Home Office
3rd Floor
Allington Towers
19 Allington Street
London SW1E 5EB

Comments may also be sent by fax to: **020 7035 5386** or by e-mail to: -
identitycards@homeoffice.gsi.gov.uk. If commenting by e-mail please include the words
"consultation response" in the subject title.

4.12   **All comments should be submitted to arrive no later than Tuesday 20th July 2004.**

Annex A

Identity Cards Bill draft clauses

Draft Identity Cards Bill

CONTENTS

DRAFT

OF A

BILL

TO

Make provision for a national scheme of registration of individuals and for the issue of cards capable of being used for identifying registered individuals; and for connected purposes.

B E IT ENACTED by the Queen's most Excellent Majesty, by and with the advice and consent of the Lords Spiritual and Temporal, and Commons, in this present Parliament assembled, and by the authority of the same, as follows:—

Registration

1 The National Identity Register

(1) It shall be the duty of the Secretary of State to establish and maintain a register of individuals (to be known as "the National Identity Register").

(2) The Register is to be established and maintained for the following purposes only ("the statutory purposes")— 5

    (a) providing a record of registrable facts about individuals in the United Kingdom;

    (b) providing a record of registrable facts about other individuals (living and dead) who have been in the United Kingdom, or who have applied to be entered in the Register; 10

    (c) facilitating the issue of cards containing information that may be used by an individual issued with one for establishing his identity, place of residence or residential status;

    (d) facilitating the provision of a service by means of which registrable facts about a registered individual may, with his consent, be ascertained or verified by other persons; and 15

    (e) enabling information recorded in the Register for any of the preceding purposes to be disclosed to persons in cases authorised by or under this Act. 20

(3) The establishment and maintenance of the Register for those purposes does not authorise—

      (a)   the use in or as regards Scotland of the Register or of a card issued in accordance with this Act, or

      (b)   the disclosure in or as regards Scotland of information recorded in the Register,

except in relation to a matter or for purposes outside the legislative competence *5* of the Scottish Parliament or in accordance with an Act of that Parliament.

  (4) In this Act "registrable fact", in relation to an individual, means—

      (a)   his identity;

      (b)   where he resides in the United Kingdom;

      (c)   where he has previously resided in the United Kingdom;   *10*

      (d)   the times at which he was resident at the different places in the United Kingdom where he has resided;

      (e)   his current residential status;

      (f)   residential statuses previously held by him;

      (g)   information about numbers allocated to him for identification purposes *15* and about the documents to which they relate;

      (h)   information about occasions on which information recorded about him in the Register has been accessed or disclosed; and

      (i)   information recorded in the Register at his request.

  (5) In this section references to an individual's identity are references to—   *20*

      (a)   his full name;

      (b)   other names by which he is or has previously been known;

      (c)   his date and place of birth and, if he has died, the date of his death; and

      (d)   physical characteristics of his that are capable of being used for identifying him.   *25*

  (6) In this section "residential status", in relation to an individual, means—

      (a)   his nationality;

      (b)   his entitlement to remain in the United Kingdom; and

      (c)   the terms and conditions of that entitlement.

2   Individuals entered in Register   *30*

  (1) An entry must be made in the Register for every individual who—

      (a)   is entitled to be entered in it; and

      (b)   applies to be entered in it.

  (2) The individuals entitled to be entered in the Register are—

      (a)   every individual who has attained the age of 16 and, without being *35* excluded under subsection (3) from an entitlement to be registered, is residing at a place in the United Kingdom; and

      (b)   every individual of a prescribed description who has resided in the United Kingdom or who is proposing to enter the United Kingdom.

  (3) Regulations made by the Secretary of State may provide that an individual *40* residing in the United Kingdom is excluded from an entitlement to be registered if he is—

      (a)   residing in the United Kingdom in exercise of an entitlement to remain there that will end less than the prescribed period after it was acquired; or   *45*

     (b)   an individual of a prescribed description who has not yet been resident in the United Kingdom for the prescribed period.

(4)   An entry for an individual may be made in the Register (whether or not he has applied to be, or is entitled to be, entered in it) if information capable of being recorded in an entry for him is otherwise available to be recorded.   5

(5)   The Secretary of State—
    (a)   may at any time modify the Register for the purpose of correcting information entered in it that he is satisfied is inaccurate; but
    (b)   is not, by virtue of any provision of this Act, to be under a duty to correct such information unless he is so satisfied.   10

(6)   An entry in the Register consisting of all the information recorded about an individual must be given a unique number, to be known as his National Identity Registration Number; and that number must comply with the prescribed requirements.

(7)   The Secretary of State may by order modify the age for the time being specified   15
in subsection (2)(a).

3   Information recorded in Register

(1)   The only information that may be recorded in the Register is—
    (a)   information the inclusion of which in an individual's entry is authorised by Schedule 1;   20
    (b)   information of a technical nature for use in connection with the administration of the Register;
    (c)   information of a technical nature for use in connection with the administration of arrangements made for purposes connected with the issue or cancellation of ID cards; and   25
    (d)   information recorded in the Register in accordance with subsection (2).

(2)   Information about an individual must be recorded in his entry in the Register (whether or not it is authorised by Schedule 1) if—
    (a)   he has made an application to the Secretary of State requesting the recording of the information as part of his entry;   30
    (b)   regulations made by the Secretary of State do not exclude it from the information that may be the subject of such a request; and
    (c)   the Secretary of State considers that it is both practicable and appropriate for it to be recorded in accordance with the applicant's request.   35

(3)   Information, once entered in the Register, may continue to be recorded in the Register for so long as it is consistent with the statutory purposes for it to be so recorded.

(4)   The Secretary of State may by order modify the information for the time being set out in Schedule 1.   40

(5)   The Secretary of State may make an order under this section adding information to the information that may be recorded in the Register only if he considers that it would be consistent with the statutory purposes for the additional information to be so recorded.

(6) The Secretary of State must not make an order containing (with or without other provision) any provision for adding information to the information that may be recorded in the Register unless a draft of the order has been laid before Parliament and approved by a resolution of each House.

4   Designation of documents for purposes of registration etc.   5

(1) The Secretary of State may by order designate a description of documents for the purposes of this Act.

(2) The only documents that may be the subject of an order designating a description of documents for the purposes of this Act are—

    (a)   documents that a person has a power or duty to issue by virtue of   10
          provision made by or under an enactment; or

    (b)   documents which a Minister of the Crown is authorised or required to issue otherwise than by virtue of provision so made.

5   Applications relating to entries in Register

(1) An application by an individual to be entered in the Register may be made   15
either—

    (a)   by being included in the prescribed manner in an application for a designated document; or

    (b)   by being submitted in the prescribed manner directly to the Secretary of State.   20

(2) Where an application to be issued with a designated document is made by an individual, the application must do one of the following—

    (a)   include an application by that individual to be entered in the Register;

    (b)   state that the individual is already entered in the Register and confirm the contents of his entry;   25

    (c)   state that the individual is entered in the Register and confirm the contents of his entry subject to the changes notified in the application.

(3) Where an individual makes—

    (a)   an application to be entered in the Register, or

    (b)   an application which for the purposes of this Act confirms (with or   30
          without changes) the contents of his entry in the Register,

the application must be accompanied by the prescribed information.

(4) Where an individual has made an application falling within subsection (3)(a) or (b), the Secretary of State may require him to do such one or more of the things specified in subsection (5) as the Secretary of State thinks fit for the   35
purpose of—

    (a)   verifying information that may be entered in the Register about that individual in consequence of that application; or

    (b)   otherwise ensuring that there is a complete, up-to-date and accurate entry about that individual in the Register.   40

(5) The things that an individual may be required to do under subsection (4) are—

    (a)   to attend at a specified place and time;

    (b)   to allow his fingerprints, and other biometric information about himself, to be taken and recorded;

    (c)   to allow himself to be photographed;   45

      (d)   otherwise to provide such information as may be required by the Secretary of State.

(6)   Regulations under this section must not require an individual to provide information to another person unless it is information required by the Secretary of State for the statutory purposes.   *5*

(7)   In this section "biometric information" and "fingerprint" have the same meanings as in paragraph 2 of Schedule 1; and the power to make consequential provision in connection with a modification of that Schedule by an order under section 3(4) includes power to make consequential modifications of subsection (5) of this section.   *10*

6   Power of Secretary of State to require registration

(1)   The Secretary of State may by order impose an obligation on individuals of a description specified in the order to be entered in the Register.

(2)   An order under this section may impose an obligation on individuals required to be entered in the Register to apply in accordance with section 5 to be so entered.   *15*

(3)   An order which imposes an obligation to make such an application must set out—
      (a)   the time when the requirement to make the application arises; and
      (b)   the period after that time within which the application must be made.   *20*

(4)   An individual who—
      (a)   contravenes an obligation imposed on him by provision made under subsections (2) and (3), or
      (b)   contravenes a requirement imposed on him under section 5(4) in connection with an application made in pursuance of such an obligation,   *25*
    shall be liable to a civil penalty not exceeding £2,500.

(5)   An individual required to be entered in the Register by virtue of this section who contravenes a requirement imposed under section 5(4) otherwise than in connection with such an application shall be liable to a civil penalty not exceeding £1,000.   *30*

(6)   An individual who has contravened an obligation imposed on him by provision made under subsections (2) and (3) and on whom a penalty has been imposed under subsection (4) in respect of that contravention shall be liable to a further civil penalty not exceeding £2,500 in respect of each subsequent occasion on which—   *35*
      (a)   a notice is given to him by the Secretary of State requiring him to make an application to be entered in the Register; and
      (b)   he fails to do so within the period specified in the notice.

7   Procedure for orders under s. 6   *40*

(1)   The Secretary of State must not make an order containing (with or without other provision) any provision for compulsory registration unless—
      (a)   a draft of the order has been laid before Parliament and approved by a resolution of each House; and

      (b)   each of the resolutions for approving the draft was agreed more than 60 days after the day on which the draft was laid before the House in question.

(2)   No draft order containing provision for compulsory registration is to be laid before Parliament unless —

      (a)   the Secretary of State has prepared and published a report containing a proposal for the making of such provision;

      (b)   the report sets out the Secretary of State's reasons for making the proposal;

      (c)   the report has been laid before Parliament and each House has approved the proposal contained in the report, either with or without modifications; and

      (d)   the draft order gives effect to the proposal so far as approved by both Houses.

(3)   An approval given in either House satisfies the requirements of subsection (2)(c) only if it was given in that House on the first occasion on which a motion for the approval of the proposal was made in that House by a Minister of the Crown after —

      (a)   the laying of the report; or

      (b)   if more than one report containing that proposal has been laid before that House, the laying of the one laid most recently.

(4)   The Secretary of State must not make an order which —

      (a)   contains (with or without other provision) any provision that he is authorised to make by section 6, but

      (b)   is not an order containing provision for compulsory registration,

unless a draft of the order has been laid before Parliament and approved by a resolution of each House.

(5)   In reckoning a period of 60 days for the purposes of subsection (1), no account shall be taken of a day for which —

      (a)   Parliament is dissolved or prorogued; or

      (b)   the House in question is adjourned as part of an adjournment of more than four days.

(6)   References in this section to provision for compulsory registration are references to any provision that the Secretary of State is authorised to make by section 6 the effect of which is to impose an obligation on individuals to be entered in the Register from a time when they would not otherwise be subject to such an obligation.

ID cards

8   Issue etc. of ID cards

(1)   For the purposes of this Act an ID card is a card which is issued to an individual by the Secretary of State, or as part of or together with a designated document, and which does one or both of the following as respects that individual —

      (a)   records registrable facts about him that are recorded as part of his entry in the Register;

      (b)   contains data enabling it to be used for facilitating the making of applications for information recorded in a prescribed part of that individual's entry in the Register, or for otherwise facilitating the disclosure of that information.

(2) An ID card issued to an individual —
  (a) must record only the prescribed information;
  (b) must record prescribed parts of it in an encrypted form; and   *5*
  (c) is valid only for the prescribed period.

(3) Except in prescribed cases, an ID card must be issued to an individual if he —
  (a) is entitled to be entered in the Register or, by virtue of section 6, is required to be so entered; and
  (b) is an individual about whom the prescribed registrable facts have been   *10* entered in the Register.

(4) In prescribed cases an ID card may be issued to an individual who —
  (a) is not required to be issued with one; but
  (b) is an individual about whom the prescribed registrable facts have been entered in the Register.   *15*

(5) An ID card relating to an individual is not to be issued except on an application made by him which either —
  (a) accompanies an application made by him to be entered in the Register; or
  (b) in the prescribed manner confirms (with or without changes) the   *20* contents of an entry already made in the Register for that individual.

(6) An application for the issue of an ID card to an individual must be included, in the prescribed manner —
  (a) in every application made by him to be issued with a designated document; and   *25*
  (b) in every application made by him in accordance with provision made under section 6.

(7) Other applications for the issue of an ID card —
  (a) may be made only in the prescribed manner;
  (b) may be made to the Secretary of State or, in prescribed cases, to a   *30* designated documents authority; and
  (c) must be accompanied by the prescribed information;
  and regulations for the purposes of paragraph (b) may authorise an application to be made to a designated documents authority irrespective of whether an application is made to that authority for the issue of a designated document.   *35*

(8) The Secretary of State must not make regulations containing (with or without other provision) any provision for prescribing —
  (a) the information to be recorded in or on an ID card, or
  (b) the form in which information is to be recorded in or on such a card,
  unless a draft of the regulations has been laid before Parliament and approved   *40* by a resolution of each House.

9   Renewal of ID cards for those compulsorily registered

(1) This section applies where an individual —
  (a) is required, by virtue of section 6, to be entered in the Register; and
  (b) is so entered.   *45*

(2) If the individual —

    (a) holds a valid ID card that is due to expire within the prescribed period, or

    (b) does not hold a valid ID card,

he must apply for one within the prescribed period.   *5*

(3) Where an individual applies for an ID card in pursuance of this section, the Secretary of State may require him to do such one or more of the things specified in subsection (4) as the Secretary of State thinks fit for the purpose of —

    (a) verifying information provided for the purposes of the application; or   *10*

    (b) otherwise ensuring that there is a complete, up-to-date and accurate entry about that individual in the Register.

(4) The things that an individual may be required to do under subsection (3) are —

    (a) to attend at a specified place and time;

    (b) to allow his fingerprints, and other biometric information about   *15* himself, to be taken and recorded;

    (c) to allow himself to be photographed;

    (d) otherwise to provide such information as may be required by the Secretary of State.

(5) An individual who contravenes —   *20*

    (a) a requirement imposed by subsection (2), or

    (b) a requirement imposed under subsection (3),

shall be liable to a civil penalty not exceeding £1,000.

(6) In this section "biometric information" and "fingerprint" have the same meanings as in paragraph 2 of Schedule 1; and the power to make   *25* consequential provision in connection with a modification of that Schedule by an order under section 3(4) includes power to make consequential modifications of subsection (4) of this section.

10 Functions of persons issuing designated documents

(1) A designated documents authority must not issue a designated document to   *30* an individual unless the authority is satisfied —

    (a) that the requirements imposed by or under this Act in relation to the application for the issue of that document to that individual have been complied with; and

    (b) that the Secretary of State has considered and disposed of so much of   *35* that application as relates to the making or confirmation of an entry in the Register.

(2) Where the designated documents authority then issues the designated document to that individual, it must ensure that the document contains, or is issued with, an ID card satisfying the prescribed requirements in relation to   *40* that individual.

(3) Regulations made by the Secretary of State may impose requirements regulating how designated documents authorities handle —

    (a) applications to be entered in the Register that are made to them;

    (b) applications to be issued with ID cards that are made to them (whether   *45* or not as part of an application for a designated document); and

(c)   applications made to them that confirm (with or without changes) an individual's entry in the Register.

(4)   Regulations made by the Secretary of State may also require designated documents authorities to notify the Secretary of State where a designated document that contains, or was issued with, an ID card —   5
(a)   is modified, suspended or revoked; or
(b)   is required to be surrendered.

Maintaining accuracy of Register etc.

11   Power to require information for validating Register

(1)   Where it appears to the Secretary of State that a person on whom a requirement   10
may be imposed under this section has in his possession information about an individual that could be used for verifying —
(a)   something recorded in that individual's entry in the Register,
(b)   something provided to the Secretary of State or a designated documents authority for the purpose of being recorded in an entry   15
about that individual in the Register, or
(c)   something otherwise available to the Secretary of State for being so recorded,
the Secretary of State may require that person to provide him with the information.   20

(2)   Where it appears to a designated documents authority —
(a)   that a person on whom a requirement may be imposed under this section has in his possession information about an individual who has applied to the authority for the issue or modification of a designated document or of an ID card, and   25
(b)   that the information could be used for verifying something that is recorded in that individual's entry in the Register or has been provided to that authority for the purpose of being recorded in an entry about that individual in the Register,
the authority may require that person to provide it with the information.   30

(3)   It shall be the duty of a person who is required to provide information under this section to comply with the requirement.

(4)   A requirement may be imposed under this section on any person specified for the purposes of this section in an order made by the Secretary of State.

(5)   The power of the Secretary of State to make an order specifying a person as a   35
person on whom a requirement may be imposed under this section includes power to provide that his duty to comply with a requirement so imposed is owed to the person imposing it and is enforceable by that person in civil proceedings —
(a)   for an injunction;   40
(b)   for specific performance of a statutory duty under section 45 of the Court of Session Act 1988 (c. 36); or
(c)   for any other appropriate remedy or relief.

(6)   The Secretary of State must not make an order containing (with or without other provision) any provision that he is authorised to make by this section   45

unless a draft of the order has been laid before Parliament and approved by a
resolution of each House.

12   Notification of changes affecting accuracy of Register

(1)   An individual to whom an ID card has been issued must notify the Secretary
       of State about —   5
          (a)   every prescribed change of circumstances affecting the information
              recorded about him in the Register; and
          (b)   every error in that information of which he is aware.

(2)   A notification for the purposes of this section must be given —
          (a)   in the prescribed manner; and   10
          (b)   within the prescribed period after the change of circumstances occurs
              or he becomes aware of the error.

(3)   Where an individual has given a notification for the purposes of this section,
       the Secretary of State may require him to do such one or more of the things
       falling within subsection (4) as the Secretary of State thinks fit for the purpose   15
       of —
          (a)   verifying the information that may be entered in the Register about that
              individual in consequence of the notified change or for the purpose of
              correcting the error; or
          (b)   otherwise ensuring that there is a complete, up-to-date and accurate   20
              entry about that individual in the Register.

(4)   The things that an individual may be required to do under subsection (3) are —
          (a)   to attend at a specified place and time;
          (b)   to allow his fingerprints, and other biometric information about
              himself, to be taken and recorded;   25
          (c)   to allow himself to be photographed;
          (d)   otherwise to provide such information as may be required by the
              Secretary of State.

(5)   Regulations under this section must not require an individual to provide
       information to another person unless it is information required by the   30
       Secretary of State for the statutory purposes.

(6)   An individual who contravenes a requirement imposed on him by or under
       this section shall be liable to a civil penalty not exceeding £1,000.

(7)   In this section "biometric information" and "fingerprint" have the same
       meanings as in paragraph 2 of Schedule 1; and the power to make   35
       consequential provision in connection with a modification of that Schedule by
       an order under section 3(4) includes power to make consequential
       modifications of subsection (4) of this section.

13   Invalidity and surrender of ID cards

(1)   Regulations may require an individual to whom an ID card has been issued to   40
       notify the Secretary of State, and such other persons as may be prescribed, if —
          (a)   the card has been lost, stolen, damaged or destroyed; or
          (b)   there is reason to suspect that the card has been tampered with.

(2)   The Secretary of State may cancel an ID card if it appears to him —

        (a)   that it was issued in reliance on inaccurate or incomplete information;

        (b)   that a change of circumstances requires a modification of the information recorded in or on it; or

        (c)   that it has been lost, stolen, damaged, destroyed or tampered with.

(3)   A person who is knowingly in possession of an ID card without either —

        (a)   the lawful authority of the individual to whom it was issued, or

        (b)   the permission of the Secretary of State,

must surrender the card as soon as it is practicable to do so.

(4)   Where it appears to the Secretary of State that a person is in possession of —

        (a)   an ID card issued to another, or

        (b)   an ID card that has expired or been cancelled or is otherwise invalid,

the Secretary of State may require that person to surrender the card within such period as he may specify.

(5)   Where an ID card has to be surrendered under subsection (3) or (4), it must be surrendered —

        (a)   to the Secretary of State; or

        (b)   in the case of a card issued by designated documents authority, either to the Secretary of State or to that authority.

(6)   A person who contravenes a requirement imposed by or under —

        (a)   any regulations under subsection (1), or

        (b)   subsection (3) or (4),

is guilty of an offence.

(7)   A person guilty of an offence under subsection (6) shall be liable —

        (a)   on summary conviction in England and Wales, to imprisonment for a term not exceeding 51 weeks or to a fine not exceeding level 5 on the standard scale, or to both;

        (b)   on summary conviction in Scotland or Northern Ireland, to imprisonment for a term not exceeding six months or to a fine not exceeding level 5 on the standard scale, or to both;

but, in relation to an offence committed before the commencement of section 281(5) of the Criminal Justice Act 2003 (c. 44), the reference in paragraph (a) to 51 weeks is to be read as a reference to six months.

(8)   Where —

        (a)   a designated document has been issued with an ID card; and

        (b)   an obligation to surrender the designated document, or otherwise to deliver it, to any person is imposed on the person with possession of it,

the obligation to surrender or otherwise to deliver the designated document includes an obligation to surrender or to deliver the ID card.

(9)   In this section —

        (a)   references to a card having been damaged include references to anything in or on it having become unreadable or otherwise unusable; and

        (b)   references to a card having been tampered with include references to information in or on it having been modified for an unlawful purpose, or copied or otherwise extracted for such a purpose.

Disclosures from Register with consent

14   Disclosures with consent of registered individual

(1) The Secretary of State may make a disclosure of information recorded in an
     individual's entry in the Register if—
     (a) an application for the disclosure is made to him by a person who has   *5*
          the authority of that individual to make the application; or
     (b) that individual otherwise consents to the making of the disclosure.

(2) The Secretary of State may by regulations make provision as to—
     (a) how an authority for the purposes of subsection (1)(a) is to be given;
     (b) the persons by whom, and the circumstances in which, an application   *10*
          for those purposes may be made; and
     (c) how such an application is to be made.

(3) Those regulations may make it a condition of making an application for the
     disclosure of information that the applicant has registered prescribed
     particulars about himself with the Secretary of State.   *15*

(4) Nothing in this section, or in any other enactment, confers on any individual—
     (a) any right to the disclosure of information recorded in so much of his
          entry in the Register as falls within paragraph 9 of Schedule 1; or
     (b) any other right in relation to that information;
     and the Secretary of State is not, in response to an application under this   *20*
     section, to make a disclosure of any information recorded in the Register unless
     he thinks fit.

(5) The power to make consequential provision in connection with a modification
     of Schedule 1 by an order under section 3(4) includes power to make
     consequential modifications of any reference in subsection (4) of this section to *25*
     paragraph 9 of that Schedule.

Required identity checks

15   Power to make public services conditional on identity checks

(1) Regulations may make provision allowing or requiring a person who provides
     a public service to make it a condition of providing the service to an individual *30*
     that the individual produces—
     (a) an ID card;
     (b) other evidence of registrable facts about himself; or
     (c) both.

(2) Regulations under this section may not allow or require the imposition of a   *35*
     condition on—
     (a) the entitlement of an individual to receive a payment under or in
          accordance with any enactment, or
     (b) the provision of any public service that has to be provided free of
          charge,   *40*
     except in cases where the individual is of a description of individuals who, by
     virtue of section 6, are required to be entered in the Register.

(3) Nothing in this section authorises the making of regulations the effect of which would be to require an individual—

    (a) to carry an ID card with him at all times; or

    (b) to produce such a card otherwise than for purposes connected with an application by him for the provision of a public service, or with the provision of a public service for which he has applied.   *5*

(4) Regulations under this section may not allow or require the imposition of a condition in or as regards Scotland on the provision of a public service except where the provision of that service is outside the legislative competence of the Scottish Parliament.   *10*

(5) References in this section and in sections 16 and 17 to the provision of a public service are references to—

    (a) the provision of any service to an individual by a public authority;

    (b) the exercise or performance in relation to an individual of any power or duty of a Minister of the Crown, the Treasury or a Northern Ireland department;   *15*

    (c) the doing by any other person of anything in relation to an individual which that person is authorised or required to do for purposes connected with the carrying out of any function conferred on him by or under an enactment; or   *20*

    (d) treating an individual as having complied with a requirement imposed on him by or under any enactment.

(6) References in this section and in section 16 to an application for the provision of a public service include references to any claim, request or requirement for the provision of the service.   *25*

16 Power to provide for checks on the Register

(1) Regulations may make provision authorising the disclosure to a person who provides a public service in respect of which—

    (a) a condition is imposed under section 15, or

    (b) a condition for the production of an ID card, or of evidence of registrable facts, or both, is imposed by or under any other enactment,   *30*

of information recorded in the Register that he requires for the purpose of ascertaining or verifying registrable facts about an individual who has applied for the provision of the service.

(2) Regulations under this section may not authorise a disclosure to be made otherwise than in accordance with regulations made by the Secretary of State under section 18.   *35*

(3) Regulations under this section may not authorise the disclosure in or as regards Scotland of any information except in relation to a matter or for purposes outside the legislative competence of the Scottish Parliament.   *40*

(4) References in this section to the provision of a public service and to applying for such a service are to be construed in accordance with section 15(5) and (6).

17 Procedure for regulations under ss. 15 and 16

(1) The power to make regulations under section 15 or 16 shall be exercisable—

      (a)   in relation to the provision of public services for which the National Assembly for Wales is responsible, by that Assembly;

      (b)   in relation to the provision of public services in Northern Ireland so far as the provision of those services is a transferred matter (within the meaning of section 4(1) of the Northern Ireland Act 1998 (c. 47)), by the Office of the First Minister and the deputy First Minister; and

      (c)   so far as not exercisable by any other person under paragraph (a) or (b), by the Secretary of State.

  (2)   Regulations containing (with or without other provision) any provision the making of which is authorised by section 15 or 16 must not be made by the Secretary of State or the Office of the First Minister and deputy First Minister unless a draft of the regulations —

      (a)   in the case of regulations made by the Secretary of State, has been laid before Parliament and approved by a resolution of each House; and

      (b)   in the case of regulations made by the Office of the First Minister and deputy First Minister, has been laid before and approved by the Northern Ireland Assembly.

  (3)   Before —

      (a)   draft regulations under section 15 or 16 are laid before either House of Parliament or the Northern Ireland Assembly, or

      (b)   regulations under that section are made by the National Assembly for Wales,

the person proposing to make the regulations must take such steps as that person thinks fit for securing that members of the public likely to be affected by the regulations are informed about the matters mentioned in subsection (4), and for consulting them about it.

  (4)   Those matters are —

      (a)   the reasons for the making of the regulations; and

      (b)   why reliance is not being placed on powers conferred otherwise than by this Act.

  (5)   Where —

      (a)   a power to impose the conditions for the provision of a public service is exercisable under any enactment not contained in this Act, and

      (b)   that power is exercisable only after consultation with such persons as may be specified or described in that enactment,

the power under section 15 or 16 to impose a condition for the provision of that service or to make provision in relation to such a condition is to be exercisable only after consultation with the persons so specified or described.

  (6)   References in this section to the provision of a public service are to be construed in accordance with section 15(5).

18   Regulations about identity checks

  (1)   The Secretary of State may by regulations make provision as to —

      (a)   the manner in which applications for disclosures authorised under section 16 must be made; and

      (b)   the information that may be disclosed in response to such an application and the manner in which it may be disclosed.

(2)   Those regulations may make it a condition of making an application for the disclosure of information, that the applicant has registered prescribed particulars about himself with the Secretary of State.

(3)   The Secretary of State must not make regulations containing (with or without other provision) any provision that he is authorised to make by this section unless a draft of the regulations has been laid before Parliament and approved by a resolution of each House.   5

(4)   Before draft regulations under this section are laid before either House of Parliament, the Secretary of State must take such steps as he thinks fit for securing that—   10
    (a)   members of the public in the United Kingdom are informed about the reasons for the proposal to make the regulations; and
    (b)   for consulting them about it.

19   Prohibition on requirements to produce identity cards

(1)   It shall be unlawful in cases not falling within subsection (2) for any person—   15
    (a)   to make it a condition of doing anything in relation to an individual that the individual establishes his identity by the production of an ID card; or
    (b)   otherwise to impose a requirement on an individual to produce such a card.   20

(2)   Each of the following is a case in which such a condition or requirement may be imposed in relation to or on an individual—
    (a)   where the condition or requirement is imposed in accordance with regulations under section 15, or in accordance with provision made by or under any other enactment;   25
    (b)   where provision is made allowing the individual to satisfy the condition or other requirement using reasonable alternative methods of establishing his identity;
    (c)   where the individual is of a description of persons who, by virtue of section 6, are required to be entered in the Register.   30

(3)   The obligation of a person by virtue of this section not to impose a condition or requirement in relation to or on an individual is a duty owed to that individual and is enforceable by him in civil proceedings—
    (a)   for an injunction or interdict; or
    (b)   for any other appropriate remedy or relief.   35

Other disclosures from Register

20   Disclosures without consent of registered individual

(1)   The Secretary of State may, without the individual's consent, make a disclosure of information recorded in an individual's entry in the Register if—
    (a)   the disclosure is authorised by this section; and   40
    (b)   any requirements imposed in relation to the disclosure by or under section 24 are complied with.

(2)   A disclosure of information is authorised by this section if it is—

(a)   a disclosure made to the Director-General of the Security Service for purposes connected with the carrying out of any of that Service's functions;

(b)   a disclosure made to the Chief of the Secret Intelligence Service for purposes connected with the carrying out of any of that Service's functions;

(c)   a disclosure made to the Director of the Government Communications Headquarters for purposes connected with the carrying out of any of the functions of GCHQ;

(d)   a disclosure made to the Director General of the National Criminal Intelligence Service for purposes connected with the carrying out of any of that Service's functions; or

(e)   a disclosure made to the Director General of the National Crime Squad for purposes connected with the carrying out of any of that Squad's functions.

(3)   A disclosure of information not falling within paragraph 9 of Schedule 1 is authorised by this section if it is made to a chief officer of police —

(a)   in the interests of national security;

(b)   for purposes connected with the prevention or detection of crime; or

(c)   for purposes specified by order made by the Secretary of State.

(4)   A disclosure of information not falling within paragraph 9 of Schedule 1 is authorised by this section if it is made to the Commissioners of Inland Revenue or the Commissioners of Customs and Excise —

(a)   in the interests of national security;

(b)   for purposes connected with the prevention or detection of crime;

(c)   for purposes connected with the prevention, detection or investigation of conduct in respect of which the Commissioners have power to impose penalties, or with the imposition of such penalties;

(d)   for the purpose of facilitating the checking of information provided to the Commissioners in connection with anything under their care and management, or with any other matter in relation to which the Commissioners have duties under any enactment;

(e)   for purposes connected with any of the functions of the Commissioners of Inland Revenue in relation to national insurance contributions or national insurance numbers; or

(f)   for other purposes specified by order made by the Secretary of State.

(5)   A disclosure of information not falling within paragraph 9 of Schedule 1 is authorised by this section if it is made to a prescribed officer of the Secretary of State's department for purposes connected with the carrying out of any prescribed functions of the Secretary of State.

(6)   A disclosure of information not falling within paragraph 9 of Schedule 1 is authorised by this section if it is made to a prescribed officer of the Department for Social Development in Northern Ireland for purposes connected with any of the functions of that Department in relation to social security benefits in Northern Ireland, or in relation to national insurance numbers.

(7)   A disclosure of information not falling within paragraph 9 of Schedule 1 is authorised by this section (so far as it is not otherwise authorised by subsections (3) to (6)) if it is made —

    (a)   for any of the purposes specified in section 17(2)(a) to (d) of the Anti-terrorism, Crime and Security Act 2001 (c. 24) (criminal proceedings and investigations); and

    (b)   otherwise than in connection with crime in or as regards Scotland in relation to a matter within the legislative competence of the Scottish Parliament.   *5*

(8)   A disclosure of information falling within paragraph 9 of Schedule 1 is authorised by this section if—

    (a)   it is made to a person to whom disclosures may be made by virtue of any of subsections (3) to (6) or is made as mentioned in subsection (7); and   *10*

    (b)   it is made for purposes connected with the prevention or detection of serious crime.

(9)   A disclosure of information to a designated documents authority is authorised by this section if it is made for any purposes connected with the exercise or performance by the authority of—   *15*

    (a)   any of its powers or duties by virtue of this Act; or

    (b)   any of its other powers or duties in relation to the issue or modification of designated documents.

(10)   Nothing in this section is to be construed as restricting any power to disclose information that exists apart from this section.   *20*

21   Supplemental provisions for s. 20

(1)   In section 20 and this section—

    "chief officer of police" means—

        (a)   the chief officer of police of a police force maintained for a police area in England and Wales;   *25*

        (b)   the chief constable of a police force maintained under the Police (Scotland) Act 1967 (c. 77);

        (c)   the Chief Constable of the Police Service of Northern Ireland;

        (d)   the Chief Constable of the Ministry of Defence Police;   *30*

        (e)   the Chief Constable of the Civil Nuclear Constabulary;

        (f)   the Chief Constable of the British Transport Police;

    "crime" means any crime within the meaning of the Regulation of Investigatory Powers Act 2000 (c. 23) (see section 81(2) of that Act) other than crime in or as regards Scotland in relation to a matter within the legislative competence of the Scottish Parliament;   *35*

    "detection", in relation to crime or serious crime, is to be construed in accordance with subsection (2);

    "GCHQ" has the same meaning as in the Intelligence Services Act 1994 (c. 13);   *40*

    "serious crime" means crime that is serious crime within the meaning of the Regulation of Investigatory Powers Act 2000 (see section 81(2) and (3) of that Act);

    "social security benefits in Northern Ireland" means benefits payable under enactments relating to social security in Northern Ireland or under the Jobseekers (Northern Ireland) Order 1995 (S.I. 1995/2705 (N.I. 15)).   *45*

(2)   Section 81(5) of the Regulation of Investigatory Powers Act 2000 (c. 23) (which
       defines detection) applies for the purposes of section 20 as it applies for the
       purposes of the provisions of that Act that are not in Chapter 1 of Part 1 of that
       Act.

(3)   Section 18 of the Anti-terrorism, Crime and Security Act 2001 (c. 24) (restriction   5
       on disclosure of information for overseas purposes) shall have effect in relation
       to a disclosure by virtue of section 20(7) as it applies in relation to a disclosure
       in exercise of a power to which section 17 of that Act applies.

(4)   The power to make consequential provision in connection with a modification
       of Schedule 1 by an order under section 3(4) includes power to make   10
       consequential modifications of any reference in section 20 to paragraph 9 of
       that Schedule.

22   Disclosures for the purpose of correcting false information

(1)   This section applies where —
       (a)   information about an individual has been provided for verification   15
             purposes (whether under section 11 or otherwise) to the Secretary of
             State or to a designated documents authority; and
       (b)   it appears to the Secretary of State that the information was false in one
             or more particulars.

(2)   The Secretary of State may, without the individual's consent, disclose to the   20
       person who provided the false information —
       (a)   the respects in which it is false; and
       (b)   what is in fact recorded in that individual's entry in respect of the
             matters to which the false information related.

(3)   A disclosure under this section is subject to compliance with any requirements   25
       imposed in relation to the disclosure by or under section 24.

(4)   The reference in this section to providing information about an individual for
       verification purposes is a reference to providing information about that
       individual that is required by the Secretary of State or a designated documents
       authority for verifying —   30
       (a)   something recorded in that individual's entry in the Register,
       (b)   something provided to the Secretary of State or a designated
             documents authority for the purpose of being recorded in an entry
             about that individual in the Register, or
       (c)   something otherwise available to the Secretary of State for being so   35
             recorded.

23   Power to authorise other disclosures without consent

(1)   In a case where there is no authorisation under section 20 or 22 for the making
       of a disclosure, the Secretary of State may nevertheless, without the
       individual's consent, make a disclosure of information recorded in an   40
       individual's entry in the Register if —
       (a)   the information is of a description specified or described in an order
             made by the Secretary of State;
       (b)   the disclosure is made to a person so specified or described;
       (c)   the disclosure is made for the purposes so specified or described; and   45

(d)   any requirements imposed in relation to the disclosure by or under section 24 are complied with.

(2)   The Secretary of State must not make an order containing (with or without other provision) any provision that he is authorised to make by this section unless a draft of the order has been laid before Parliament and approved by a resolution of each House.

5

24   Rules for making disclosures without consent

(1)   The Secretary of State may make a disclosure under sections 20 to 23 of information falling within paragraph 2 of Schedule 1 only if he is satisfied that it would not have been reasonably practicable for the person to whom the disclosure is made to have obtained the information by other means.

10

(2)   The Secretary of State may by regulations make provision —
    (a)   imposing requirements that must be satisfied before a disclosure is made under any of sections 20 to 23; and
    (b)   restricting the persons who may be authorised to act on his behalf for or in connection with the making of such a disclosure.

15

(3)   Those regulations may include —
    (a)   provision requiring a disclosure to be made to a person only where an application for it has been made by or on behalf of that person;
    (b)   provision specifying or describing the persons who may make applications on that person's behalf; and
    (c)   provision imposing other requirements as to the manner in which such applications must be made.

20

(4)   The Secretary of State may also, by regulations, provide that a disclosure that may be made to a person specified in or under any of sections 20 to 23 may be made instead to a person who —
    (a)   is authorised by the specified person to be a recipient of such disclosures;
    (b)   holds such office, rank or position as may be specified in the regulations; and
    (c)   is under the direction or control of the specified person, or is otherwise answerable or subordinate to him, in respect of any of his duties as a person holding that office, rank or position.

25

30

National Identity Scheme Commissioner

25   Appointment of Commissioner

35

(1)   The Prime Minister must appoint a Commissioner to be known as the National Identity Scheme Commissioner.

(2)   It shall be the function of the Commissioner to keep under review the exercise by the Secretary of State of his powers under this Act to disclose information recorded in the Register without the consent of the individual to whom it relates.

40

(3)   It shall be the duty of every official of the Secretary of State's department to provide the Commissioner with all such information (including information

recorded in the Register) as he may require for the purpose of carrying out his function under this Act.

(4)   A person is not to be appointed as the Commissioner unless he holds or has held high judicial office (within the meaning of the Appellate Jurisdiction Act 1876 (c. 59)).   *5*

(5)   The Commissioner is to hold office in accordance with the terms of his appointment; and there shall be paid to him out of money provided by Parliament such allowances as the Treasury may determine.

(6)   The Secretary of State —
        (a)   after consultation with the Commissioner, and   *10*
        (b)   subject to the approval of the Treasury as to numbers,
       must provide the Commissioner with such staff as the Secretary of State considers necessary for the carrying out of the Commissioner's functions.

26   Reports by Commissioner

(1)   As soon as practicable after the end of each calendar year, the Commissioner   *15*
       must make a report to the Prime Minister about the carrying out of the Commissioner's functions.

(2)   The Commissioner may also, at any other time, make such report to the Prime Minister on any matter relating to the carrying out of those functions as the Commissioner thinks fit.   *20*

(3)   The Prime Minister must lay before Parliament a copy of every annual report made to him under subsection (1).

(4)   If it appears to the Prime Minister, after consultation with the Commissioner, that the publication of a particular matter contained in an annual report would be contrary to the public interest or prejudicial to —   *25*
        (a)   national security,
        (b)   the prevention or detection of crime,
        (c)   the economic well-being of the United Kingdom, or
        (d)   the continued discharge of the functions of any public authority,
       the Prime Minister may exclude that matter from the copy of the report that he   *30*
       lays before Parliament.

(5)   Where a matter is excluded under subsection (4) from a copy of an annual report laid before Parliament, the Prime Minister must, when he lays that copy of the annual report, also lay before Parliament a statement that a matter has been excluded from the report under that subsection.   *35*

Offences

27   Possession of false identity documents etc.

(1)   It is an offence for a person to have in his possession or under his control —
        (a)   an identity document that is false and that he knows or believes to be false,   *40*
        (b)   an identity document that was improperly obtained and that he knows or believes to have been improperly obtained, or
        (c)   an identity document that relates to someone else,

with the intention of using it for establishing registrable facts about himself, or of allowing or inducing another to use it for establishing, ascertaining or verifying registrable facts about himself or about any other person (with the exception, in the case of a document within paragraph (c), of the individual to whom it relates).

(2) It is an offence for a person to make, or to have in his possession or under his control—

    (a) any machine or other apparatus which, to his knowledge, is or has been specially designed or adapted for the making of false identity documents, or

    (b) any article or material which, to his knowledge, is or has been specially designed or adapted to be used in the making of false identity documents,

with the intention that he or another will make a false identity document and that the document will be used by somebody for establishing, ascertaining or verifying registrable facts about a person.

(3) It is an offence for a person to have in his possession or under his control, without reasonable excuse—

    (a) an identity document that is false;

    (b) an identity document that was improperly obtained;

    (c) an identity document that relates to someone else; or

    (d) any machine or other apparatus, article or material which, to his knowledge, is or has been specially designed or adapted for the making of false identity documents or to be used in the making of such documents.

(4) A person guilty of an offence under subsection (1) or (2) shall be liable, on conviction on indictment, to imprisonment for a term not exceeding ten years or to a fine, or to both.

(5) A person guilty of an offence under subsection (3) shall be liable—

    (a) on conviction on indictment, to imprisonment for a term not exceeding two years or to a fine, or to both;

    (b) on summary conviction in England and Wales, to imprisonment for a term not exceeding twelve months or to a fine not exceeding the statutory maximum, or to both;

    (c) on summary conviction in Scotland or Northern Ireland, to imprisonment for a term not exceeding six months or to a fine not exceeding the statutory maximum, or to both;

but, in relation to an offence committed before the commencement of section 154(1) of the Criminal Justice Act 2003 (c. 44), the reference in paragraph (b) to twelve months is to be read as a reference to six months.

(6) For the purposes of this section—

    (a) an identity document is false only if it is false within the meaning of Part 1 of the Forgery and Counterfeiting Act 1981 (c. 45) (see section 9(1) of that Act); and

    (b) an identity document was improperly obtained if false information was provided, in or in connection with the application for its issue or an application for its modification, to the person who issued it or (as the case may be) to a person entitled to modify it;

and references to the making of a false identity document include references to the modification of an identity document so that it becomes false.

(7)   In this section "identity document" has the meaning given by section 28.

28   Identity documents for the purposes of s. 27

(1)   In section 27 "identity document" means any document that is, or purports to be —

    (a)   an ID card;

    (b)   a designated document;

    (c)   an immigration document;

    (d)   a United Kingdom passport (within the meaning of the Immigration Act 1971 (c. 77));

    (e)   a passport issued by or on behalf of the authorities of a country or territory outside the United Kingdom or by or on behalf of an international organisation;

    (f)   a document that can be used (in some or all circumstances) instead of a passport;

    (g)   a UK driving licence; or

    (h)   a driving licence issued by or on behalf of the authorities of a country or territory outside the United Kingdom.

(2)   In subsection (1) "immigration document" means —

    (a)   a document used for confirming the right of a person under the Community Treaties in respect of entry or residence in the United Kingdom;

    (b)   a document which is given in exercise of immigration functions and records information about leave granted to a person to enter or to remain in the United Kingdom; or

    (c)   a registration card (within the meaning of section 26A of the Immigration Act 1971);

and in paragraph (b) "immigration functions" means functions under the Immigration Acts (within the meaning of the Asylum and Immigration (Treatment of Claimants, etc.) Act 2004).

(3)   In that subsection "UK driving licence" means —

    (a)   a licence to drive a motor vehicle granted under Part 3 of the Road Traffic Act 1988 (c. 52);

    (b)   a licence to drive a motor vehicle granted under Part 2 of the Road Traffic Act (Northern Ireland) 1981 (S.I. 1981/154 (N.I. 1)); or

    (c)   a document issued as a counterpart with a licence falling within paragraph (a) or (b).

(4)   The Secretary of State may by order modify the list of documents in subsection (1).

(5)   The Secretary of State must not make an order containing (with or without other provision) any provision that he is authorised to make by subsection (4) unless a draft of the order has been laid before Parliament and approved by a resolution of each House.

29 Unauthorised disclosure of information

(1) A person is guilty of an offence if, without lawful authority, he discloses information which is or has become available to him by reason of his holding an office or employment the duties of which relate, in whole or in part, to —

    (a) the establishment or maintenance of the Register; or

    (b) the issue, modification, cancellation or surrender of ID cards.

(2) For the purposes of this section a disclosure is made with lawful authority if, and only if —

    (a) it is authorised by or under this Act or any other enactment;

    (b) it is made in pursuance of an order or direction of a court or of a tribunal established by or under any enactment;

    (c) it is made in pursuance of a Community obligation; or

    (d) it is made for the purpose of performing the duties of an office or employment of the sort mentioned in subsection (1).

(3) It is a defence for a person charged with an offence under this section to show that, at the time of the alleged offence, he believed, on reasonable grounds, that he had lawful authority to make the disclosure in question.

(4) A person guilty of an offence under this section shall be liable, on conviction on indictment, to imprisonment for a term not exceeding two years or to a fine, or to both.

30 Providing false information

(1) A person is guilty of an offence if, in circumstances falling within subsection (2), he provides false information to any person —

    (a) for the purpose of securing the making or modification of an entry in the Register;

    (b) in confirming an entry in the Register; or

    (c) for the purpose of obtaining for himself or another the issue or modification of an ID card.

(2) Those circumstances are that, at the time of the provision of the information he —

    (a) knows or believes the information to be false; or

    (b) is reckless as to whether or not it is false.

(3) A person guilty of an offence under this section shall be liable —

    (a) on conviction on indictment, to imprisonment for a term not exceeding two years or to a fine, or to both;

    (b) on summary conviction in England and Wales, to imprisonment for a term not exceeding twelve months or to a fine not exceeding the statutory maximum, or to both;

    (c) on summary conviction in Scotland or Northern Ireland, to imprisonment for a term not exceeding six months or to a fine not exceeding the statutory maximum, or to both;

but, in relation to an offence committed before the commencement of section 154(1) of the Criminal Justice Act 2003 (c. 44), the reference in paragraph (b) to twelve months is to be read as a reference to six months.

31   Tampering with Register

(1)   In section 3 of the Computer Misuse Act 1990 (c. 18) (unauthorised modification of computer material) —

    (a)   in paragraph (b) of subsection (7) (penalty for offence on conviction on indictment), at the beginning insert "subject to subsection (8)"; and   *5*

    (b)   after that subsection insert the subsection set out in subsection (2) of this section.

(2)   The inserted subsection is —

    "(8)   Where an offence under this section is committed wholly or partly in relation to any contents of a computer that consist of the National   *10* Identity Register or any part of it, subsection (7)(b) above shall have effect as if for 'five years' there were substituted 'ten years'."

32   Consequential amendments relating to offences

(1)   In Schedule 1A to the Police and Criminal Evidence Act 1984 (c. 60) (arrestable offences), at the end insert —   *15*

"Identity Cards Act 2004

    28   An offence under —

        (a)   section 27(3) of the Identity Cards Act 2004 (possession of false document etc.);

        (b)   section 29 of that Act (disclosure of information on National   *20* Identity Register); or

        (c)   section 30 of that Act (providing false information)."

(2)   In section 1(2) of the Criminal Justice Act 1993 (c. 36) (Group A offences in respect of which jurisdiction is extended for some purposes in relation to conduct outside England and Wales), after paragraph (c) insert —   *25*

    "(ca)   section 27 of the Identity Cards Act 2004;".

(3)   At the end of Article 26(2) of the Police and Criminal Evidence (Northern Ireland) Order 1989 (S.I. 1989/1341 (N.I. 12)) (offences for which an arrest may be made without a warrant), insert —

    "(l)   An offence under —   *30*

        (i)   section 27(3) of the Identity Cards Act 2004 (possession of false document etc.);

        (ii)   section 29 of that Act (disclosure of information on National Identity Register); or

        (iii)   section 30 of that Act (providing false information)."   *35*

(4)   In Article 38(2) of the Criminal Justice (Northern Ireland) Order 1996 (S.I. 1996/3160 (N.I. 24)) (which makes provision in relation to conduct outside Northern Ireland corresponding to that made by section 1(2) of the Criminal Justice Act 1993), after sub-paragraph (c) insert —

    "(ca)   section 27 of the Identity Cards Act 2004;".   *40*

Civil penalties

33 Imposition of civil penalties

(1) This section applies where the Secretary of State is satisfied that a person ("the defaulter") is a person who is liable under this Act to a civil penalty not exceeding a specified amount.   *5*

(2) The Secretary of State may, by a notice given to the defaulter in the prescribed manner, impose on him a penalty of such amount, not exceeding the specified amount, as the Secretary of State thinks fit.

(3) A notice imposing such a penalty must—

    (a) set out the Secretary of State's reasons for deciding that the defaulter is *10* liable to a penalty;

    (b) state the amount of the penalty that is being imposed;

    (c) specify a date before which the penalty must be paid to the Secretary of State;

    (d) describe how payment may be made;   *15*

    (e) explain the steps that the defaulter may take if he objects to the penalty; and

    (f) set out and explain the powers of the Secretary of State to enforce the penalty.

(4) The date for the payment of a penalty must be not less than 14 days after the *20* giving of the notice imposing it.

(5) A penalty imposed in accordance with this section—

    (a) must be paid to the Secretary of State in a manner described in the notice imposing it; and

    (b) if not so paid by the specified date, is to be recoverable by him *25* accordingly.

(6) In proceedings for recovery of a penalty so imposed no question may be raised as to—

    (a) whether the defaulter was liable to the penalty; or

    (b) the amount of the penalty.   *30*

(7) Sums received by the Secretary of State in respect of penalties imposed in accordance with this section must be paid into the Consolidated Fund.

34 Objection to penalty

(1) A person to whom a notice under section 33 has been given may give notice to the Secretary of State that he objects to the penalty on one or both of the *35* following grounds—

    (a) that he is not liable to it;

    (b) that the amount of the penalty is too high.

(2) The notice of objection—

    (a) must set out the grounds of the objection and the objector's reasons for *40* objecting on those grounds; and

    (b) must be given to the Secretary of State in the prescribed manner and within the prescribed period after the giving of the notice imposing the penalty.

(3) The Secretary of State must consider a notice of objection given in accordance with this section and may then—

    (a) cancel the penalty;

    (b) reduce it;

    (c) increase it; or   5

    (d) confirm it.

(4) The Secretary of State must not enforce a penalty in respect of which he has received a notice of objection before he has notified the objector of the outcome of his consideration of the objection.

(5) That notification of the outcome of his consideration must be given, in the   *10* prescribed manner—

    (a) before the end of the prescribed period; or

    (b) within such longer period as he may agree with the objector.

(6) Where, on consideration of an objection, the Secretary of State increases the penalty, he must give the objector a new penalty notice under section 33; and,   *15* where he reduces it, he must notify the objector of the reduced amount.

35   Appeals against penalties

(1) A person on whom a penalty has been imposed under section 33 may appeal to the court on one or both of the following grounds—

    (a) that he is not liable to it; or   *20*

    (b) that the amount of the penalty is too high.

(2) An appeal under this section must brought within such period after the giving of the notice imposing the penalty to which it relates as may be specified by rules of court.

(3) On an appeal under this section, the court may—   *25*

    (a) allow the appeal and cancel the penalty;

    (b) allow the appeal and reduce the penalty; or

    (c) dismiss the appeal.

(4) An appeal under this section shall be by way of a rehearing of the Secretary of State's decision to impose the penalty.   *30*

(5) The matters to which the court may have regard when determining an appeal under this section include all matters that the court considers relevant, including—

    (a) matters of which the Secretary of State was unaware when he made his decision; and   *35*

    (b) matters which (apart from this subsection) the court would be prevented from having regard to by virtue of rules of court.

(6) An appeal under this section may be brought in relation to a penalty irrespective of whether a notice of objection under section 34 has been given in respect of that penalty and of whether there has been an increase or reduction   *40* under that section.

(7) In this section "the court" means—

    (a) in England and Wales or Northern Ireland, a county court; and

    (b) in Scotland, the sheriff.

36   Code of practice on penalties

(1)   The Secretary of State must issue a code of practice setting out the matters that he will consider when determining the amount to be imposed in any case by way of a civil penalty under this Act.

(2)   The Secretary of State must have regard to the code when—   5
   (a)   imposing a civil penalty under this Act; or
   (b)   considering a notice of objection under section 34.

(3)   The court must have regard to the code when determining any appeal under section 35.

(4)   Before issuing the code, the Secretary of State must lay a draft of it before   10
Parliament.

(5)   The code issued under this section does not come into force until the time specified by order made by the Secretary of State.

(6)   The Secretary of State may from time to time—
   (a)   revise the whole or a part of the code; and   15
   (b)   issue the revised code.

(7)   Subsections (4) and (5) apply to a revised code as they apply to the code first issued under this section.

Supplemental

37   Fees etc.   20

(1)   The Secretary of State may by regulations specify fees, of such amounts as he thinks fit, to be paid to him in respect of each of the following—
   (a)   applications made to him for an entry to be made in the Register, for the modification of an entry or for the issue of an ID card;
   (b)   the making or modification of entries in the Register;   25
   (c)   the issue of ID cards;
   (d)   applications for the disclosure to any person of the whole, or a part, of the information contained in any one or more entries in the Register;
   (e)   the making of such a disclosure;
   (f)   applications for the confirmation of any information by reference to   30
information recorded in the Register;
   (g)   the issue of such a confirmation.

(2)   The consent of the Treasury is required for the making of regulations under subsection (1).

(3)   Every power conferred by or under an enactment to fix or impose fees in   35
respect of—
   (a)   an application for a designated document, or
   (b)   the issue of a designated document,
includes power to fix or impose fees in respect of anything done by virtue of this Act in connection with such an application, or with the issue of such a   40
document.

(4)   Fees received by the Secretary of State by virtue of this section must be paid
      into the Consolidated Fund.

38   Orders and regulations

(1)   Every power conferred by this Act on the Secretary of State or the National
      Assembly for Wales to make an order or regulations is a power exercisable by   *5*
      statutory instrument.

(2)   The power of the Office of the First Minister and deputy First Minister to make
      regulations under section 15 or 16 is a power exercisable by statutory rule for
      the purposes of the Statutory Rules (Northern Ireland) Order 1979 (S.I. 1979/
      1573 (N.I. 12)).   *10*

(3)   Subject to subsection (5), a statutory instrument containing an order or
      regulations made by the Secretary of State under this Act shall be subject to
      annulment in pursuance of a resolution of either House of Parliament.

(4)   Subject to subsection (5), every power conferred by this Act on a person to
      make an order or regulations includes power—   *15*
      (a)   to make different provision for different cases;
      (b)   to make provision subject to such exemptions and exceptions as that
            person thinks fit; and
      (c)   to make such incidental, supplemental, consequential and transitional
            provision as that person thinks fit.   *20*

(5)   Subsection (3) does not apply to a statutory instrument which—
      (a)   comprises an order under section 41 bringing a provision of this Act
            into force; or
      (b)   makes provision by reference to which a draft of the order or
            regulations contained in the instrument is required to have been laid   *25*
            before Parliament and approved by a resolution of each House;
      and subsection (4) does not apply to the power to make an order under section
      41 bringing a provision of this Act into force.

39   Expenses of Secretary of State

There shall be paid out of money provided by Parliament—   *30*
      (a)   any sums authorised or required to be paid by the Secretary of State for
            or in connection with the carrying out of his functions under this Act;
            and
      (b)   any increase attributable to this Act in the sums which are payable out
            of money so provided under any other Act.   *35*

40   General interpretation

(1)   In this Act—
            "card" includes a document or other article, or a combination of a
                  document and an article, in or on which information is or may be
                  recorded;   *40*
            "the Commissioner" means the National Identity Scheme Commissioner
                  appointed under section 25;
            "contravention" includes a failure to comply, and cognate expressions are
                  to be construed accordingly;

"confirm", in relation to an individual's entry in the Register, is to be construed in accordance with subsection (3);

"designated document" means a document of a description designated for the purposes of this Act by an order under section 4;

"designated documents authority" means a person with the power or duty to issue a designated document;   5

"document" includes a stamp or label;

"enactment" includes—

    (a)   a provision of Northern Ireland legislation; and

    (b)   enactments passed or made after the passing of this Act;   10

"false", in relation to information, includes containing any inaccuracy or omission that results in a tendency to mislead;

"ID card" is to be construed in accordance with section 8(1);

"information" includes documents and records;

"issue", in relation to a document or card, and cognate expressions are to   15 be construed in accordance with subsection (2);

"modification" includes omission, addition or alteration, and cognate expressions are to be construed accordingly;

"prescribed" means prescribed by regulations made by the Secretary of State;   20

"place of residence" and "resides" are to be construed subject to any regulations under subsection (4);

"public authority" has the same meaning as in section 6 of the Human Rights Act 1998 (c. 42);

"the Register" means the National Identity Register established and   25 maintained under section 1;

"registrable fact" has the meaning given by section 1(4);

"statutory purposes" means the purposes specified in section 1(2).

(2)   References in this Act to the issue of a document or card include references to its renewal, replacement or re-issue (with or without modifications).   30

(3)   References in this Act to an individual confirming the contents of his entry in the Register are references to his confirming that entry to the extent only that it consists of information falling within paragraphs 1 to 5 of Schedule 1 or section 3(2).

(4)   The Secretary of State may by regulations make provision for the purposes of   35 this Act as to the circumstances in which a place is to be regarded, in relation to an individual—

    (a)   as a place where he resides; or

    (b)   as his principal place of residence in the United Kingdom.

(5)   The power to make consequential provision in connection with a modification   40 of Schedule 1 by an order under section 3(4) includes power to make consequential modifications of any reference in subsection (3) of this section to paragraphs 1 to 5 of that Schedule.

41   Short title, repeals, commencement and extent

(1)   This Act may be cited as the Identity Cards Act 2004.   45

(2)   The enactments in Schedule 2 are repealed to the extent shown in the second column of that Schedule.

(3)   This Act (apart from this section) shall come into force on such day as the Secretary of State may by order appoint; and different days may be appointed for different purposes.

5

(4)   This Act extends to Northern Ireland.

SCHEDULES

SCHEDULE 1   Section 3

INFORMATION THAT MAY BE RECORDED IN REGISTER

Personal information

1   The following may be recorded in an individual's entry in the Register —   5
        (a)   his full name;
        (b)   other names by which he is or has been known;
        (c)   his date of birth;
        (d)   his place of birth;
        (e)   his gender;   10
        (f)   the address of his principal place of residence in the United Kingdom; and
        (g)   the address of every other place in the United Kingdom where he has a place of residence.

Identifying information   15

2   (1)   The following may be recorded in an individual's entry in the Register —
        (a)   a photograph of his head and shoulders;
        (b)   his fingerprints; and
        (c)   other biometric information about him.

   (2)   In this paragraph —   20
       "biometric information", in relation to an individual, means data about his external characteristics, including, in particular, the features of an iris or of any other part of the eye; and
       "fingerprint", in relation to an individual, means a record (in any form and produced by any method) of the skin pattern and other   25 physical characteristics or features of any of his fingers.

Residential status

3   The following may be recorded in an individual's entry in the Register —
        (a)   his nationality;
        (b)   his entitlement to remain in the United Kingdom; and   30
        (c)   the terms and conditions of that entitlement.

Personal reference numbers etc.

4   (1)   The following may be recorded in an individual's entry in the Register —
        (a)   his National Identity Registration Number;

(b)   the number of any ID card issued to him;

(c)   any national insurance number allocated to him;

(d)   the number of any immigration document relating to him;

(e)   the number of any United Kingdom passport (within the meaning of the Immigration Act 1971 (c. 77)) that has been issued to him;

(f)   the number of any passport issued to him by or on behalf of the authorities of a country or territory outside the United Kingdom or by or on behalf of an international organisation;

(g)   the number of any document that can be used by him (in some or all circumstances) instead of a passport;

(h)   the number of any identity card issued to him by the authorities of a country or territory outside the United Kingdom;

(i)   any reference number allocated to him by the Secretary of State in connection with an application made by him for permission to enter or to remain in the United Kingdom;

(j)   the number of any work permit (within the meaning of the Immigration Act 1971) relating to him;

(k)   the number of any designated document which is held by him and is a document the number of which does not fall within any of the preceding sub-paragraphs; and

(l)   the date of expiry or period of validity of a document the number of which is recorded by virtue of this paragraph.

(2)   In this paragraph "immigration document" means—

(a)   a document used for confirming the right of a person under the Community Treaties in respect of entry or residence in the United Kingdom;

(b)   a document which is given in exercise of immigration functions and records information about leave granted to a person to enter or to remain in the United Kingdom; or

(c)   a registration card (within the meaning of section 26A of the Immigration Act 1971);

and in paragraph (b) "immigration functions" means functions under the Immigration Acts (within the meaning of the Asylum and Immigration (Treatment of Claimants, etc.) Act 2004).

Record history

5   The following may be recorded in an individual's entry in the Register—

(a)   information falling within the preceding paragraphs that has previously been recorded about him in the Register;

(b)   particulars of changes affecting that information and of changes made to his entry in the Register; and

(c)   his date of death.

Registration history

6   The following may be recorded in an individual's entry in the Register—

(a)   the date of every application for registration made by him;

(b)   the date of every application by him for a modification of the contents of his entry;

     (c)   the date of every application by him confirming the contents of his entry (with or without changes);

     (d)   particulars (in addition to its number) of every ID card issued to him;

     (e)   whether each such card is in force and, if not, why not; and

     (f)   particulars of any other individual who has countersigned an application by the individual in question for an ID card or a designated document, so far as those particulars were included on the application. 5

Validation information

7   The following may be recorded in the entry in the Register for an individual— 10

     (a)   the information provided in connection with every application by him to be entered in the Register, for a modification of the contents of his entry or for the issue of an ID card;

     (b)   the information provided in connection with every application by him confirming his entry in the Register (with or without changes); 15

     (c)   particulars of the steps taken in connection with any application mentioned in paragraph (a) or (b) or otherwise for identifying the applicant or for verifying the information provided in connection with the application; 20

     (d)   particulars of any other steps taken or information obtained (otherwise than in connection with an application mentioned in paragraph (a) or (b)) for ensuring that there is a complete, up-to-date and accurate entry about that individual in the Register;

     (e)   particulars of every notification given by that individual for the purposes of section 12; 25

     (f)   particulars of every notification given by that individual for the purposes of regulations under section 13(1); and

     (g)   particulars of any requirement by the Secretary of State to a person to surrender an ID card issued to that individual. 30

Security information

8   The following may be recorded in the entry in the Register for an individual—

     (a)   a personal identification number to be used for facilitating the making of applications for, and the disclosure of, information recorded in his entry; 35

     (b)   a password or other code to be used for that purpose; and

     (c)   questions and answers to be used for identifying a person seeking to make such an application or to apply for or to make a modification of that entry. 40

Access records

9   The following may be recorded in the entry in the Register for an individual—

     (a)   particulars of every occasion on which a person has accessed the individual's entry and of the person who accessed it; 45

    (b)   particulars of every occasion on which information contained in the individual's entry has been disclosed, of the disclosure and of the person to whom it was disclosed;

    (c)   particulars of every step taken on such an occasion for modifying the individual's entry, for issuing or cancelling an ID card issued to him or for requiring the surrender of such a card; and   5

    (d)   information for identifying the person who took any such steps on such an occasion.

SCHEDULE 2

Section 41

REPEALS

10

Short title and chapter	Extent of repeal
Forgery and Counterfeiting Act 1981 (c. 45)	In section 5— (a) subsection (5)(f) and (fa); and (b) subsections (9) to (11).
Asylum and Immigration (Treatment of Claimants, etc.) Act 2004	Section 3.

15

Annex B

Explanatory Notes on the draft clauses

1. These draft explanatory notes relate to the draft Identity Cards Bill. They have been prepared by the Home Office in order to assist the reader of the draft Bill and to help inform debate on it. They do not form part of the draft Bill.

2. The notes need to be read in conjunction with the draft Bill. They are not, and are not meant to be, a comprehensive description of the draft Bill. So where a clause or part of a clause does not seem to require any explanation or comment, none is given.

SUMMARY AND BACKGROUND

3. In July 2002, the Government launched a consultation on Entitlement Cards and Identity Fraud (Cm 5557). The consultation period lasted until 31st January 2003. A summary of findings from the consultation exercise was published on 11th November 2003, *Identity Cards* (Cm 6019). The detailed Government's response to the Consultation Points was placed on the Home Office website.

4. At the same time as publication of the findings, the Government announced its decision to build a base for a compulsory national identity cards scheme. The Identity Cards: the Next Steps (Cm 6020) document sets out in more detail how the Government would proceed. The draft Identity Cards Bill gives effect to the Government's proposals for the introduction of identity cards throughout the United Kingdom as set out in Identity Cards: the Next Steps.

5. There is currently no legislation providing for UK identity cards. The main features of the legal framework needed to introduce identity cards are:

    *   the creation of a National Identity Register of basic personal information;
    *   a family of ID cards based on designated identity documents and new types of identity card;

- powers for card issuing organisations to verify data supplied by an applicant to process applications for cards;

- disclosure of National Identity Register information to law enforcement and security agencies in specified circumstances;

- criminal offences and civil sanctions required to make the scheme effective;

- enabling organisations to use the card to facilitate provision of services by allowing identity to be verified; and

- the power to set a date in the future when registration for an identity card will be compulsory subject to a special super-affirmative process.

OVERVIEW OF THE STRUCTURE

6.   The draft Bill deals with nine topics:

- Registration
- ID cards
- Maintaining accuracy of Register etc.
- Disclosures from Register with consent
- Required identity checks
- Other disclosures from Register
- National Identity Scheme Commissioner
- Offences
- Civil penalties

TERRITORIAL EXTENT AND TERRITORIAL APPLICATION

7.   The identity cards scheme needs to operate on a UK-wide basis to deal with matters over which the UK Parliament retains exclusive control, notably, immigration.

8.   The draft legislation allows the devolved administrations in Wales and Northern Ireland to make Regulations making the production of an ID card a condition of providing a public service for which these administrations are responsible. The identity cards scheme is not intended to be applicable in Scotland in relation to matters that are within the legislative competence of the Scottish Parliament (in particular in relation to public services and criminal matters that are within that competence). Any such use would require authorisation by an Act of the Scottish Parliament.

9.   The draft legislation for identity cards creates new offences. As these offences relate to documents or databases that operate on a UK basis, they will be applicable throughout the UK.

COMMENTARY ON CLAUSES

Registration

Clause 1: The National Identity Register

10.   This clause establishes the National Identity Register for the identity cards scheme and sets out the purposes of the Register.

11.   Subsection (2) provides that the Register is only for specified purposes, the "statutory purposes". These specified purposes consist of recording personal information known as "registrable facts" about categories of individuals, issuing cards, facilitating the provision of services by allowing identity to be verified, and allowing disclosure of information in certain circumstances.

12.   Subsection (3) makes it clear that neither the Register nor identity cards may be used for purposes within the legislative competence of the Scottish Parliament. This is subject to provision made by an Act of that Parliament.

13.   Subsections (4) to (6) give further explanation of what is meant by personal information. This, in particular, means name, date and place of birth, nationality, immigration status, address, physical characteristics of a person that are capable of being used for identification purposes (e.g. biometric information), information included at a person's request; and historical records of this personal information.

14.   Biometric information is defined in Schedule 1 in relation to an individual as data about his external characteristics. Examples include iris patterns and fingerprints. This schedule also includes other information which may be held on the Register as explained in paragraph 20. Parliamentary consent is required to add further information to that Schedule.

Clause 2: Individuals entered in Register

15.   This clause sets out who may be entered on to the Register and the Secretary of State's duty to make arrangements to enable these entries to be made.

16.   Subsection (2) sets out the individuals who are entitled to be entered on the Register. These include individuals who have attained the age of 16 and are residing in the UK. They also include individuals of a description prescribed in Regulations made by the Secretary of State who have resided in the UK, or who are proposing to enter the UK. Subsection (3) gives the Secretary of State power, by Regulations, to exclude individuals from the entitlement to be entered on the Register if they do not meet prescribed requirements in relation to time of residence in the UK. The age of 16 mentioned previously may be varied by secondary legislation as provided for in subsection (7). In general, an entry on the Register must be made if an application is made and the person is entitled to be entered (subsection (1)).

17.   Subsection (4) provides that in some circumstances, a person who has not applied or is not entitled may be entered into the Register. For example, this power would allow the entry on to the Register of a failed asylum seeker who had not applied for an ID card but whose information including biometric data was available. This means that if he applies to stay in the UK again using a different identity, his previous status as a failed asylum seeker will have been recorded. This subsection does not constitute a power to record the biometric data of a person in the first place.

18.   Subsection (5) allows the information held on the Register to be corrected.

19.   Subsection (6) provides for every person registered on the Register to be assigned a unique number, the National Identity Registration Number to be attached to the information recorded about an individual. The format of the National Identity Registration Number is to be specified in Regulations. Other personal reference numbers may be recorded on the Register as provided for in Schedule 1, paragraph 4.

Clause 3: Information recorded in Register

20.   Clause 3 sets out the information that may be recorded in the Register. Subsection (1) provides that information may be recorded only if it is included in Schedule 1, if it is otherwise necessary for the administration of the scheme, or if it is provided for in subsection (2). Schedule 1 may be amended by secondary legislation following a resolution

in both Houses of Parliament (subsections (4)-(6)) to add to the list of information that may be recorded on the Register. However, any additional information must be consistent with the statutory purposes of the scheme. So, for example, this power to amend Schedule 1 could not be used to include criminal records in that Schedule without further primary legislation as recording previous criminal convictions is not within the statutory purposes of the scheme or the definition of registrable facts.

21.   Subsection (2) enables other information to be recorded if an individual has asked for it to be included and the Secretary of State agrees. For example, an individual may ask for emergency contact details to be included on the Register.

22.   Subsection (3) allows information to be kept for as long as it is consistent with the statutory purposes for it to be so kept, which in practice is likely to be indefinitely. This will make verification of individuals easier by ensuring an audit trail of changes is made, so a person changing information held on the Register to avoid detection would be identified. This would also enable the Register to retain information of individuals who had died or left the country and thereby prevent fraudulent use of these identities. This is in line with Clause 1(2)(b) which includes as one of the statutory purposes of the Register, providing a record of registrable facts of people who have been in the UK (living and dead). Under Clause 1(3) this information may only be used or disclosed in Scotland in relation to reserved matters.

Clause 4: Designation of documents for purposes of registration etc.

23.   Clause 4 provides for the Secretary of State to have the power by order to designate documents for the purposes of the draft Bill, for example, passports. Documents so designated will become part of the ID cards scheme. These documents are referred to in the draft Bill as "designated documents". Persons responsible for issuing designated documents are referred to in the draft Bill as "designated documents authorities".

24.   Subsection (2) provides that the Secretary of State may only designate documents which are issued under an enactment or which a Minister of the Crown is otherwise authorised or required to issue, for example, passports or residence permits. This means that only documents issued by the public sector may be designated by the Secretary of State. None of these provisions prevents other organisations from being involved in the issuing process however. For example, private sector organisations may have certain parts of the process contracted out to them, such as actual production of the card. Although if this involved disclosure of information on the Register then this will need to be authorised under the draft Bill.

Clause 5: Applications relating to entries in Register

25. Clause 5 sets out how an application for entry to the Register should be made.

26. Subsection (1) provides that an application can be made by being included in an application for a designated document or by being submitted directly to the Secretary of State.

27. Under subsection (2), if an application for a designated document is submitted, then the application must also include one of the following:

   • an application to be entered in the Register;
   • confirmation that the individual is already registered and confirming his entry;
   • confirmation that the individual is already registered and notifying changes to his entry.

   For example, if passports were designated documents, an individual in applying for a passport must at the same time include an application to be entered in the Register if he is not already entered in the Register or else confirm his entry. In practice, information on the designated document application form is likely to include all the information needed to create an entry on the Register or to verify an existing entry.

28. Subsection (3) provides that an application for registration or confirmation of entry should be accompanied by such information as may be prescribed by the Secretary of State. The information required may vary for different categories of person. For example, third country nationals may be required to provide information regarding their immigration status.

29. Under subsection (4) the Secretary of State may make further requirements of applicants in order to verify information to be entered on the Register and keep that information up to date, for example, in cases of doubt or suspected fraud.

30. Subsection (5) expands on what an individual applying to be entered in the Register or confirming his entry in the Register may be required to do under subsection (4). This includes attending in person, agreeing to be photographed, allowing biometric information to be recorded, or providing any other information that may be required by the Secretary of State. The meaning of "biometric information" and "fingerprint" is the same as that provided in paragraph 2 of Schedule 1. An order under Clause 3(4) that amends that paragraph may include consequential amendments of subsection (5).

31.   Subsection (6) ensures that information may not be required by Regulations under this clause unless it is for the statutory purposes of the scheme. This is to ensure that there is no expansion in the scope of the information held on the Register without the consent of Parliament.

Clause 6: Power of Secretary of State to require registration

32.   This clause provides a power to require an individual to apply to register. The ID cards scheme will be introduced in two stages. Initially it will not be compulsory to register although in applying for a designated document from the time that that document is designated, it will be compulsory to register or confirm an entry already made (see Clause 5). If the conditions were right, it is intended to make registration compulsory, whether or not a person applies for a designated document. See Cm 6020, Identity Cards: the Next Steps.

33.   Immigration Rules may already include a requirement for foreign nationals to obtain a document, such as a residence permit. However, if the Government wished for a requirement to make an application to be made under the draft Identity Cards Bill, for example to allow the applicant's details to be recorded in the Register, the Government would first have to designate the document under Clause 4 and then make it a requirement for foreign nationals to register under Clause 6.

34.   Subsection (1) provides a power for the Secretary of State to make registration compulsory. This power would apply regardless of whether a person applies for a designated document (for which an application to register or be registered is a requirement as soon as the document is so designated). However, this power does not extend to requiring people to produce ID cards on demand. This subsection provides the facility to phase in the compulsory registration, for example, so that different categories of persons are required to register by different dates. It may be, for instance, that people over a certain age may initially or permanently be excluded from the requirement to register. It might also be compulsory, for example, for a third country national to register before such time as the scheme becomes compulsory for European Economic Area or UK nationals.

35.   Subsection (2) ensures that in making registration compulsory, the order to do so may include an obligation on individuals to apply for registration in accordance with Clause 5. The order will also set a future date by which people included in the order should have made an application (subsection (3)).

36.   Subsection (4) provides that the maximum penalty for failure to register when required to do so or for contravening a requirement under Clause 5(4) (i.e. not providing the further

information required by the Secretary of State) in connection with an obligation under Clause 6 would be a civil penalty of up to £2,500.

37.   Subsection (5) provides that a person who contravenes a requirement imposed under Clause 5(4) other than in connection with an application required under Clause 6, is liable to a civil penalty of up to £1,000. This penalty is for those people who are required to and do register but then fail to provide the information required by the Secretary of State to keep the Register up to date.

38.   Where an individual fails to satisfy his obligation under subsections (2) and (3), he is liable for a further civil penalty not exceeding £2,500 in respect of each time the Secretary of State gives him notice requiring him to make an application and he fails to do so before the set deadline.

Clause 7: Procedure for orders under s6

39.   This clause sets out the procedures for the "super-affirmative" process which would apply to compulsory registration. This means that if the Government decides that it wishes to make registration compulsory, whether or not a person applies for a designated document, it must proceed in the following stages:

- The Government must publish in a report its reasons for wanting to make registration compulsory, including a proposal for how compulsion will operate (subsection (2)(a) and (b));
- Both Houses of Parliament must debate and vote on the proposal and they may modify the proposal (subsection (2)(c));
- The Government would lay a draft order consistent with the proposal approved by both Houses;
- The draft order so laid would then need to be approved by both Houses (subsection (1) and subsection (2)(d));
- If either House did not approve the proposal or the Government was not content with the proposal as modified by either House, it must start the process again with a fresh report and proposal if it decides to make the case again for a move to compulsion (subsection (3));
- If the Government wishes to make changes to the compulsion order which do not have the effect of "increasing" the degree of compulsion, for example, lowering the age beyond which it would not be compulsory to register, it does not need to go through the "super-affirmative" process again (subsection (4)).

40. Subsection (5) sets out how the calculation should be made of the 60 days required between the laying and approving of the draft order mentioned above.

41. Subsection (6) defines the term compulsory registration.

ID cards

Clause 8: Issue etc. of ID cards

42. This clause sets out the procedure for issuing ID cards.

43. The identity cards scheme will involve the issuing of an ID card to every person registered as entitled to remain in the United Kingdom for longer than a specified period. A number of different documents will be capable of qualifying as an ID card. These other cards will be designated as ID cards by the Secretary of State. "ID cards" in this draft Bill is used as the generic family name and is defined under this clause.

44. Subsection (1) explains that an ID card is a card which holds personal information as recorded on the National Identity Register as well as data enabling the card to be used for obtaining access to the individual's entry on the Register, for example, a personal identification number. An ID card may form part of a designated document or be a separate card issued as an ID card.

45. Subsection (2) establishes that cards will contain data which is legible on the face of the card itself and data contained in the card. It ensures that the card must only hold specific information as set out in Regulations.

46. This subsection also provides that the ID card will have a limited validity. Different validity periods may be specified for different categories of person, for example, an elderly person's ID card may remain valid for the rest of his life without the need for reconfirmation, whereas a foreign national's may be linked to the length of authorised stay. Subsection (3) requires that except in prescribed cases ID cards must be issued to individuals who are entitled to be, and whose personal information has been, entered on the Register. However, there are special cases where someone who is not required to be issued with an ID card may be issued with an ID card providing registrable facts about him have been entered in to the Register (subsection (4)).

47.   Subsection (5) provides that an ID card will only be issued once an application has been made and sufficient information has been provided for the individual to be entered on the Register or an existing entry is confirmed.

48.   Under subsection (6) an application for a designated document must include an application for an ID card in the manner prescribed. Where an application for registration is made in pursuance of a requirement under Clause 6 (compulsory registration), the application must also include an application for an ID card in the prescribed manner. In practice, the application form for a designated document will contain the information required to make an application for an ID card rather than requiring two separate application forms to be completed.

49.   Subsection (7) ensures that any other application for an ID card must be in the prescribed manner, and should be made to the Secretary of State or in certain circumstances to a designated documents authority and with the prescribed information.

50.   In the case of a designated documents authority, an application for an ID card may in certain circumstances be made separately from any application for the designated document. This allows a designated documents authority to issue an ID card that is not part of or issued with a designated document.

51.   Regulations specifying the information that may be recorded in or on an ID card or the form in which the information is to be recorded need the agreement of Parliament via affirmative resolution.

Clause 9: Renewal of ID cards for those compulsorily registered

52.   This clause provides for the renewal of cards for those individuals who are required by Clause 6 of the draft Bill to be entered into the Register.

53.   Subsection (2) makes it a requirement for individuals whose card will expire in the prescribed period or whose card is not valid to apply for an ID card within the prescribed period.

54.   Subsection (3) gives the Secretary of State the power to require an individual applying for an ID card under this clause to do certain things so that the Secretary of State can verify the information provided and ensure the accuracy of the Register. Subsection (4) sets out what

these requirements might be and includes personal attendance, the recording of biometric information, being photographed and providing such other information as may be required. "Biometric information" and "fingerprint" have the same meaning as provided in Schedule 1, paragraph 2. The powers to amend that paragraph under Clause 3(4) includes a power to make consequential amendments to subsection (4).

55.   An individual who fails to renew is liable to a civil penalty not exceeding £1,000 (subsection (5)).

Clause 10: Functions of persons issuing designated documents

56.   A designated documents authority is an issuer of a designated document. This clause sets out how common standards will be set for all designated documents authorities in carrying out their functions in relation to the Register and ID cards.

57.   Subsection (1) requires that a designated document may only be issued if the designated documents authority is satisfied that:

- all requirements of the draft Bill in relation to the application that was made for the designated document have been satisfied (for example, the application for the designated document included an application to be entered in the Register); and
- the Secretary of State has considered and disposed of so much of the application for the designated document as required to make or confirm an entry in the Register.

58.   Subsection (2) requires that a designated document may only be issued if the designated document contains, or is issued with, an ID card which satisfies the prescribed requirements in relation to the individual in question, for example, that it records prescribed information on the face of the card.

59.   Subsection (3) sets out in more detail the requirements that may be imposed on designated documents authorities, regarding:

- how applications made to them for entry on the Register are to be handled;
- how applications to be issued with ID cards made to them are to be handled, whether they be stand-alone applications or made with applications for designated documents; and

- how applications made to them confirming an individual's entry to the Register are to be handled.

60. Subsection (4) allows the Secretary of State to make Regulations requiring those issuing designated documents to notify the Secretary of State where a designated document is modified, suspended or revoked; or required to be surrendered. For example, if a passport is a designated document and is subsequently required to be surrendered for bail purposes, the National Identity Register will need to be informed to "disable" an ID card that was issued as part of, or together with, the passport.

Maintaining accuracy of Register etc.

Clause 11: Power to require information for validating Register

61. This clause deals with the provisions necessary to permit data to be shared with the Secretary of State and designated documents authorities for the purposes of verifying information to be placed or which is currently placed on the National Identity Register where no such powers already exist. This is specifically about ensuring the accuracy of the Register and it does not confer the power to share data for wider purposes; neither does it allow the Secretary of State or a designated documents authority to request information that is not relevant for the purposes of validating the Register. Under this draft Bill, Parliament will have to approve each "gateway" via an affirmative order.

62. Subsection (1) places a duty on a person to provide information to the Secretary of State for the purposes of verifying an individual's entry to the Register. Subsection (2) extends this obligation to disclose specified information to those bodies given the function of issuing cards, the designated document authorities. This obligation is mandatory (subsection (3)) and over-rides other obligations under which the person may hold that information.

63. Subsection (4) sets out that the requirement may be imposed on any person specified for the purposes in an order. This could include for example, private sector, local government or central government organisations. The order making provision to require information is subject to the affirmative resolution procedure (subsection (6)).

64. Subsection (5) provides a power that orders to require a person to provide information may be enforced via civil court proceedings.

Clause 12: Notification of changes affecting accuracy of Register

65.   This clause sets out how changes in circumstances should be notified in order to maintain the accuracy of the Register.

66.   Subsection (1) places a person registered under a duty to notify the Secretary of State of any change in his circumstances that may be prescribed, for example this might be change of address or change of name, and notify the Secretary of State of every error in the information held about him that he is aware of. This will enable the Register to maintain accurate information. The notification procedures are to be set out in Regulations (subsection (2)).

67.   Further information may be required to verify the information that may be entered as a consequence of the notification or to ensure that the entry is up to date (subsection (3)). This requirement to provide further information may include personal attendance, being photographed, allowing biometric information to be recorded or otherwise providing information. Again "fingerprint" and "biometric information" is as defined in paragraph 2 of Schedule 1 and the power to modify that paragraph by an order under Clause 3(4) includes a power to make consequential amendments to this subsection (4). The information that may be required by Regulations under this clause may only be required if it is consistent with the statutory purposes (subsection (5)).

68.   Subsection (6) provides that the maximum penalty for failure to comply with a requirement under this clause is a civil penalty of £1,000.

69.   Section 99 (4) of the Road Traffic Act 1988 provides for a criminal offence where the holder of a driving licence fails to update changes to the name or address on a driving licence. This offence is unchanged by the provisions of this draft Bill.

Clause 13: Invalidity and surrender of ID cards

70.   This clause covers invalidity and surrender of ID cards.

71.   Subsection (1) provides that Regulations can prescribe the manner in which the fact that an ID card has been lost, stolen, damaged or destroyed, or that there is reason to suspect that the card has been tampered with, must be reported. If a card was issued based on inaccurate information, requires modification or has been lost, stolen, damaged, destroyed or tampered with, then it may be cancelled (subsection (2)).

72.   Subsection (3) provides that if a person is in possession of an ID card which does not belong to them, without the individual's to whom the card was issued lawful authority or permission from the Secretary of State, he must surrender it.

73.   The Secretary of State may require a person to surrender an ID card that is not his or is invalid within such period as the Secretary of State may specify (subsection (4)).

74.   It is an offence not to surrender in these circumstances and an offender is liable to imprisonment or a fine or both (subsections (6) and (7)).

75.   Subsection (8) ensures that where there is an obligation to surrender a designated document, the ID card that has been issued with it must also be surrendered. For example, if a passport is a designated document, any obligation to surrender a passport also includes an obligation to surrender the ID card part of the passport as well as the booklet or any separate ID card that was issued with the passport.

Disclosures from Register with Consent

Clause 14: Disclosures with consent of registered individual

76.   This clause enables the provision of an identity verification service with the consent of the individual.

77.   Subsection (1) gives the Secretary of State the power to disclose information recorded in any entry, provided that the individual has consented to his details on the Register being checked, or the application is made by a person who has been authorised by the individual to make the application for disclosure.

78.   Subsection (2) provides a power to make Regulations prescribing how this authority is to be given, the persons who can make an application and in what circumstances an application may be made and how an application can be made. These Regulations may include a requirement that to make an application for the disclosure of information, the applicant must have first registered certain details with the Secretary of State (subsection (3)).

79.   Subsection (4) excludes the information held within Schedule 1, paragraph 9 (the access records of the entry to the Register) being disclosed even with consent under this clause. It also provides that the Secretary of State must only disclose information if he thinks fit. So,

the Secretary of State may refuse to disclose information even where the consent of the registered person has been given. For example, if an organisation had misused disclosed information (e.g. passing it on without proper authorisation to a third party), the Secretary of State may refuse to disclose any further information to that organisation.

Required identity checks

Clause 15: Power to make public services conditional on identity checks

80.   Identity Cards – the next steps (Cm 6020) sets out two objectives for the use of identity cards in relation to public services. These were to simplify checks on eligibility for services and to reduce fraudulent use of services. This clause provides a power to make this link between the identity cards scheme with the provision of public services in cases where existing powers may be deficient. Subsection (5) defines what is meant by the provision of a public service. This is broadly defined and is not restricted to what might be commonly understood as "public services" such as the NHS.

81.   Subsection (1) provides a power to make Regulations which allow or require a person who provides a public service to make it a condition of providing the service that an individual produces an ID card and/or other evidence of his registrable facts.

82.   Subsection (2) ensures that Regulations made under subsection (1) cannot make it mandatory to produce an identity card or information which can be verified against the National Identity Register in order to receive payments provided under legislation or any service provided free of charge before it is compulsory for that individual to register (under Clause 6). This means that we cannot make it mandatory for a person to produce a card, for example to access social security benefits or free NHS treatment, until it is compulsory for that person to register (under Clause 6).

83.   Subsection (3) specifically excludes the possibility of the carrying of cards being made compulsory. This includes both the carrying of a card and its production on demand other than for the purposes of an application for a public service.

84.   Subsection (4) provides that the powers under this clause do not extend to public services provided in Scotland that are within the legislative competence of the Scottish Parliament. If the Scottish Parliament wishes to make production of a card a condition of provision of

those services, it would first have to pass an Act of that Parliament to remove the "lock" in Clause 1(3).

85.   Subsection (6) defines what is meant by an application for the provision of a public service.

Clause 16: Power to provide for checks on the Register

86.   This clause provides a power to enable checks to be made of information recorded in the Register by people providing public services.

87.   Subsection (1) provides a power to disclose to a person providing a public service for which Regulations under Clause 15 have been made or in respect to which any other legislation makes it a condition to produce an ID card or any other evidence of registrable facts recorded on the Register, information recorded in the Register. This must be for the purposes of ascertaining or verifying information of an individual applying for the public service.

88.   Disclosure must be in accordance with Regulations made under Clause 18. This clause does not authorise disclosures in relation to matters in or as regards Scotland that are within the legislative competence of the Scottish Parliament. If the Scottish Parliament wishes to pass equivalent legislation to make Regulations about identity checks, it would have to remove the "lock" in Clause 1(3). The Scottish Parliament would also have to define what is meant by "public service" in Scotland for the purposes of required identity checks in its legislation.

Clause 17: Procedure for regulations under ss. 15 and 16

89.   This clause sets out the procedure for making Regulations under Clauses 15 and 16, including how this will apply to devolved administrations.

90.   Subsection (1) sets out who may make Regulations under Clauses 15 and 16. Where the provision of public services is the responsibililty of the National Assembly for Wales, only that Assembly may make Regulations under Clauses 15 and 16. Where the provision of public services is transferred to Northern Ireland, then the First Minister and Deputy First Minister only may make Regulations. Where this power is not exercisable by any other person, the Secretary of State may make regulations.

91. Regulations made under Clause 15 or 16 must be approved by a resolution in both Houses of Parliament in the case of Regulations made by the Secretary of State; and in the case of Regulations in Northern Ireland, they must be laid before and approved by the Northern Ireland Assembly (subsection (2)).

92. Under subsection (3), before any Regulations are made there must be steps taken for ensuring that members of the public are informed and consulted on the proposal. Subsection (4) provides that this must include the reasons for the proposal and why existing provisions are not sufficient.

93. Subsection (5) requires there to be consultation with interested parties, for example the providers of a public service, before any Regulations are made under Clause 15 or 16 if there is an equivalent requirement in other legislation to consult these interested parties.

Clause 18: Regulations about identity checks

94. This clause gives the Secretary of State the power to regulate identity checks under Clause 16.

95. Subsection (1) provides that Regulations under Clause 18 may specify the manner in which applications for checks of the Register are to be made and the manner in which a disclosure is to be made.

96. Subsection (2) provides that an application for disclosure may be made dependent on the applicant registering with the Secretary of State as may be prescribed.

97. The Regulations are subject to an affirmative resolution procedure. Before any draft Regulations are laid before Parliament, the Secretary of State must take steps to ensure that members of the public are informed and consulted on any proposals.

Clause 19: Prohibition on requirements to produce identity cards

98. This clause makes clear that there may be no requirement on individuals by organisations to produce an ID card as the only acceptable proof of identity before a move to compulsion under Clause 6, other than in the circumstances set out in subsection (2) including where a requirement is made under Clause 15.

99.   Subsection (1) makes it unlawful for any person to demand an ID card as a condition of doing anything to an individual e.g. providing a service.

100. The exceptions to this are set out in subsection (2). These include where there is a specific requirement under Clause 15 or in accordance with provisions under another enactment; where the organisation allowed for reasonable alternative methods of proving identity; or when it is compulsory for that individual to register.

101. Subsection (3) makes clear that this prohibition in subsection (1) may be enforced by the individual in the civil court.

Other disclosures from Register

Clause 20: Disclosures without consent of registered individual

102. This clause provides the power to disclose specified information held on the Register to specified persons for specified purposes without the consent of the registered person. Subsection (1) provides a power for this disclosure so long as it is authorised in this clause and Clause 24 is complied with.

103. Subsection (2) provides that information may be disclosed to specified bodies for their purposes.

104. Subsection (3) provides a power to disclose information not specified within paragraph 9 of Schedule 1 to a Chief Officer of police, for the purposes as set out in subsection (3). This excludes disclosure in relation to crimes in or as regards Scotland that are matters within the legislative competence of the Scottish Parliament. Paragraph 9 of Schedule 1 concerns information about how a card is used or a Register entry is accessed as opposed to the "static" information held on the Register, such as place and date of birth, about the registered person.

105. A similar power is provided in subsection (4) for the disclosure of information to the Commissioners of Inland Revenue or the Commissioners of Customs and Excise, except that falling within paragraph 9 of Schedule 1, for the purposes set out in subsection (4).

106. Where information does not fall within paragraph 9 of Schedule 1, disclosure of that information is permitted if it is made to a prescribed officer of the Secretary of State's

department in order to carry out prescribed functions of the Secretary of State (subsection (5)). This allows for the disclosure of information to other parts of Government which are the responsibility of a Secretary of State, e.g. to the Department for Work and Pensions. As social security benefits in Northern Ireland are a transferred matter, when devolution is restored they will not be the responsibility of a Secretary of State and so specific provisions need to be made. Subsection (6) enables the disclosure to extend to prescribed officers of the Department for Social Development in Northern Ireland in connection with social security benefits or national insurance numbers.

107. Under subsection (7) where a disclosure of information is made for any of the purposes specified in sections 17(2)(a) to (d) of the Anti-terrorism, Crime and Security Act 2001 (disclosing information for the purposes of criminal investigations or proceedings overseas), it is authorised under this clause but only subject to Clause 24. Subsection (7) does not authorise disclosures in relation to crimes in or as regards Scotland that are matters within the legislative competence of the Scottish Parliament.

108. Disclosure of information falling within paragraph 9 of Schedule 1, which is the access records of the Register entry, is authorised if it is to certain specified persons or is made for purposes authorised by subsection (7) and for the purposes connected with preventing or detecting serious crime. This allows a higher threshold to apply depending on the sensitivity of information being disclosed.

109. "Serious crime" is defined in Clause 21 as crime that (a) involves the use of violence, results in substantial financial gain or is conducted by a large number of persons in pursuit of a common purpose, or (b) the offence or one of the offences is an offence for which a person who has attained the age of twenty-one and has no previous convictions could reasonably be expected to be sentenced to imprisonment for a term of three years or more. In these cases, specified organisations may also have disclosed to them information held in paragraph 9 of Schedule 1 on access records.

110. Subsection (9) extends disclosure of information to a designated documents authority if the disclosure is made for any purposes connected with powers or duties by virtue of this draft Bill or those in relation to the issue or modification of designated documents.

111. Subsection (10) ensures that this clause does not restrict powers existing elsewhere to disclose information.

Clause 21: Supplemental provisions for s. 19

112.   Subsection (1) defines terms used in Clause 20.

113.   Subsection (2) defines detection with reference to existing legislation. Subsection (3) allows the Secretary of State to prohibit the disclosure of information on the Register by virtue of Clause 19(7) in overseas proceedings as specified in section 18 of the Anti-terrorism, Crime and Security Act 2001.

114.   Subsection (4) makes sure that any changes authorised by Parliament to the Schedule specifying what can be held on the Register are reflected in what can be disclosed under Clause 20.

Clause 22: Disclosures for the purpose of correcting false information

115.   This clause provides a power to disclose information from the Register to a person or organisation who has supplied information to help verify an entry in the Register where information provided proved to be inaccurate.

116.   Subsection (1) sets out the circumstances in which disclosure under this clause applies. Subsection (2) provides a power to disclose to the person providing the information any discrepancies between it and the information recorded on the Register, provided that Clause 24 is complied with.

117.   Subsection (4) defines what is meant by providing information about an individual for verification purposes.

Clause 23: Power to authorise other disclosures without consent

118.   This clause provides that the Secretary of State may make a disclosure of information without consent in any circumstances where an order has been made specifying or describing the information, to a person so specified or described, for purposes so specified or described and any requirements under Clause 24 are complied with. This order is subject to an affirmative resolution procedure.

Clause 24: Rules for making disclosures without consent

119.   Subsection (1) provides that a disclosure under Clauses 20 to 23 may only be authorised where the Secretary of State is satisfied that it was not reasonably practicable for the person to have obtained the information by another means. For example, if fingerprint information is recorded on the Register, the police would first have to search their own fingerprint records before resorting to the Register.

120.   Subsections (2) to (4) allow the Secretary of State to make Regulations imposing requirements before any disclosure is made, restricting those who may be authorised to act on his behalf in connection with the making of such a disclosure and providing to whom a disclosure may be made instead of a person specified under Clauses 20 to 23.

National Identity Scheme Commissioner

Clause 25: Appointment of Commissioner

121.   This clause establishes a Commissioner to oversee the practice of disclosure of information held on the Register.

122.   The Prime Minister is under the duty to appoint a National Identity Scheme Commissioner under subsection (1). Subsection (2) sets out the functions of the Commissioner.

123.   It is the duty of every official in the Secretary of State's department to provide the information the Commissioner requires to carry out his function (subsection (3)).

124.   In order to be appointed as Commissioner, a person must hold or have held high judicial office. The Commissioner should hold office in accordance with the terms of his appointment and provisions should be made for him to be paid such allowances as the Treasury may determine out of money provided by Parliament.

125.   Under subsection (6) the Secretary of State is under a duty, after consultation with the Commissioner, and subject to the approval of the Treasury as to numbers, to provide the Commissioner with such staff as the Secretary of State considers necessary for the carrying out of the Commissioner's functions.

Clause 26: Reports by Commissioner

126. Under subsection (1) the Commissioner is under a duty to report each year to the Prime Minister, who is himself under a duty to lay before Parliament that report subject to certain exceptions set out in subsection (4) and following the procedures in subsection (5).

127. There is also provision for the Commissioner to report at any other time regarding any matter related to the carrying out of his functions.

Offences

Clause 27: Possession of false identity documents etc.

128. This clause creates new criminal offences related to possessing false identity documents and mirrors existing offences contained in the Forgery and Counterfeiting Act 1981.

129. Subsection (1) sets out the circumstances under which a person is guilty of an offence where he has knowledge or belief that a document is either false or has been improperly obtained, or where he is in possession of a document that relates to someone else. To be guilty of the offence the person must intend that the document be used for an improper purpose.

130. Subsection (2) makes it illegal to make or possess equipment used for making false identity documents with the intention that the equipment will be used for making false identity documents which in turn will be used for improper purposes. Subsection (4) sets out the maximum penalties for such offences.

131. Subsection (3) makes it an offence for a person to have in his possession, without reasonable excuse, a false or improperly obtained document, a document relating to someone else, or equipment used for making false identity documents. These offences apply irrespective of any intent to use the documents or equipment. This is an offence which was not provided for previously in the Forgery and Counterfeiting Act 1981. Subsection (5) sets out penalties for such an offence.

132. Subsection (6) defines what is meant by "false" and limits this definition to this clause. Subsection (6) also defines what is meant by "improperly obtained" and "making" a false identity document. Subsection (7) makes clear the "identity document" is defined in Clause 28.

Clause 28: Identity documents for the purposes of s. 27

133.   Subsection (1) defines what is meant by an "identity document". This list may be amended by an order subject to an affirmative resolution procedure (subsections (4) and (5)).

134.   Subsection (2) defines what is meant by an "immigration document".

135.   Subsection (3) defines what is meant by a "UK driving licence".

Clause 29: Unauthorised disclosure of information

136.   This clause creates a new criminal offence of unlawful disclosure of information held on the National Identity Register.

137.   Subsection (1) sets out the circumstances under which a person is guilty of such an offence.

138.   Subsection (2) defines what is meant by "lawful authority" for the purposes of this clause.

139.   Subsection (3) states that a person has a defence if he can show that he believed, on reasonable grounds, that he had lawful authority to disclose the information.

140.   Subsection (4) sets out the maximum penalties for the offence.

Clause 30: Providing false information

141.   This clause creates a new offence of providing false information for purposes connected with the Register or an ID card.

142.   For the purposes of this clause, false is defined in Clause 40. Subsections (1) and (2) set out the circumstances under which a person is guilty of such an offence. Subsection (3) sets out maximum penalties for such an offence.

Clause 31: Tampering with Register

143.   This clause deals with cases where someone modifies information held on the Register to falsify it. This would already be an offence under the Computer Misuse Act 1990, however it would only attract a maximum penalty of 5 years. As making a false entry on the Register is the equivalent of making a false ID card, the maximum penalty in these circumstances is increased to 10 years in line with the penalty for the false ID card offence in Clause 27(4).

Clause 32: Consequential amendments relating to offences

144.   Subsection (1) makes the offences under Clauses 27(3), 29 and 30 arrestable in England and Wales. Subsection (3) extends this to Northern Ireland.

145.   Subsection (2) extends the usual jurisdiction of the courts in England and Wales for the offences in Clause 27. Subsection (4) extends the usual jurisdiction of the courts in Northern Ireland for the offences in Clause 27.

Civil penalties

Clause 33: Imposition of civil penalties

146.   This clause sets out the way in which civil penalties under the ID cards scheme will operate.

147.   Where the Secretary of State is satisfied that the person is liable to a civil penalty as set out in the draft Bill, the Secretary of State may issue in the prescribed manner a notice to the defaulter, setting out why the penalty is being imposed, the amount of the penalty, the date by which the penalty must be paid, how payment should be made, setting out the steps the defaulter may take if he objects and finally explaining the powers to enforce the penalty (subsection (3)).

148.   The date by which the payment must be made cannot be less than 14 days after the notice is issued (subsection (4)).

149.   The penalty imposed by this clause, must be paid in the manner described by the notice and if it is not paid, the amount is recoverable by the Secretary of State via the civil courts. When recovering the penalty no question may be raised as to whether the defaulter was liable to the penalty or as to the amount of the penalty.

Clause 34: Objection to penalty

150. Clause 34 sets out the steps to be taken if the recipient of the notice objects.

151. A recipient of a notice may give notice to the Secretary of State that he objects to the penalty. This must include what he objects to and why. This "notice of objection" must be made in the prescribed manner and before a date to be prescribed (subsections (1) and (2)).

152. If this procedure is complied with, the Secretary of State will determine whether or not to: cancel the penalty; reduce it; increase it; confirm it (subsection (3)). The Secretary of State must not enforce a penalty of which he has received a notice of objection, until he has considered the objection.

153. This notification of outcome must be given in the prescribed manner, by a prescribed date or if the objector agrees by the end of a longer period.

154. If, after consideration, the Secretary of State increases the penalty, a new notice must be issued under Clause 33. If the penalty is reduced, the objector must be notified accordingly.

Clause 35: Appeals against penalties

155. This clause sets out the process of appealing against penalties. A person does not have to object to a penalty under Clause 34 before making an appeal to the court under this clause.

156. The grounds of the appeal are set out in subsection (1). Subsection (2) ensures that there will be a time limit to any appeal.

157. The appeal will be a re-hearing of the decision of the Secretary of State to impose a penalty (subsection (4)). Under subsection (5) the court may consider all matters it considers relevant.

158. The court may decide to cancel the penalty, reduce the penalty or uphold the penalty under subsection (3).

159. Subsection (7) specifies which courts may hear an appeal.

Clause 36: Code of practice on penalties

160.   This clause sets out the provisions relating to the code of practice on penalties.

161.   The Secretary of State has the duty to issue a code of practice setting out the matters that will be considered when determining the amount of a civil penalty. He must have regard to the code when imposing a penalty or considering a notice of objection. A court must also have regard to the code when determining any appeal.

162.   Before issuing the code, a draft must be laid before Parliament. It then comes into force as specified by order.

Supplemental

Clause 37: Fees etc

163.   This clause makes provision for the payment of fees.

164.   Subsection (1) enables fees to be set for:

- applications;
- modification of an entry;
- issue of ID cards;
- applications for disclosure of any part of the information contained on the Register;
- making of such a disclosure;
- applications for confirmation of any information recorded; and
- the issue of such a confirmation.

165.   The fee setting powers in existing legislation governing designated documents remain unchanged. However, subsection (3) allows for the fees for designated documents to cover the costs of dealing with matters under this draft Bill (i.e. the Register and ID cards) when those matters are dealt with in relation to applications for, and the issuing of, designated documents.

Clause 38: Orders and regulations

166.   This clause provides how Orders and Regulations are to be made. In general this will be through a negative resolution procedure except in cases specifically provided for in the draft Bill.

167.   Subsection (4) enables provisions to be varied for different cases, with exemptions and exceptions. For example, Regulations may allow different application procedures for groups such as the very elderly or those with mental health problems.

Clause 39: Expenses of Secretary of State

168.   This clause deals with how expenses of the Secretary of State are to be paid.

Clause 40: General interpretation

169.   This clause provides for interpretation of defined terms in the draft Bill.

Clause 41: Short title, repeals, commencements and extent

170.   This clause allows the preceding provisions of the draft Bill to be brought into force by order made by the Secretary of State.

171.   The draft Bill extends to Northern Ireland.

Schedule 1

172.   Schedule 1 sets out the information that may be recorded in the Register. This includes:

* personal information – names, date and place of birth, gender, addresses;
* identifying information – photograph, fingerprint, other biometric information;
* residential status – nationality, entitlement to remain, terms and conditions of that entitlement;

- personal reference numbers – for example the National Identity Registration Number and other government issued numbers, and validity periods of related documents;
- record history – historical information previously recorded, audit trail of changes and date of death;
- registration history – dates of application, changes to information, dates of confirmation, information regarding other ID cards already issued, details of counter-signatures;
- validation information – information provided for any application, modification, confirmation or issue and other steps taken in connection with an application or entry, details of any requirement to surrender;
- security information – personal identification numbers, password or other codes, and questions and answers that could be used to identify a person seeking access; and
- access records – the audit trail of when an entry was:
  - accessed and by whom;
  - disclosed and to whom;
  - steps taken modifying an entry;
  - steps taken issuing, cancelling or for requiring surrender of a card; and
  - who undertook these.

Schedule 2

173. Repeals can be found in Schedule 2 to the draft Bill.

FINANCIAL EFFECTS OF THE BILL

174. The initial start up costs for the identity cards scheme will be met from existing Departmental budgets.

175. The expectation is that, when the scheme is established, overall running costs will be covered by overall charges for the application and issue of cards and for identity verification services provided by the scheme.

176. The Government's intention is that cards would be issued free to 16 year olds, and reduced-fee cards would be available to those on low incomes. Everyone else will pay a standard charge. The charge will be either an increase on the fee for a designated document (such as a passport or driving licence) or just a straight fee for the plain Identity Card. People who have both a passport and a driving licence would only pay the uplift once

(i.e. it would not apply to both documents). Building on existing systems will give more opportunities for keeping additional costs down as some of the activities needed for the Identity Cards Scheme are already carried out by agencies like DVLA and the UK Passport Service as part of their current procedures.

177. Most people will join the scheme when they apply for or renew their driving licence or passport for which charges are already levied. The minimum charge to obtain a 10-year passport from UK Passport Service is £42 and the full cost of obtaining an initial 10-year driving licence from DVLA is £38. In practice the cost that many people currently pay for these documents is around £8-£10 higher when taking account of the cost of photographs and services that check that forms have been completed correctly and the right documentation enclosed. These costs would be included in a national identity cards scheme.

178. If the Government did not implement a scheme which covered everyone but concentrated purely on implementing more secure passports and driving licences including biometrics, initial estimates suggest that the 10 year cost of passports would rise to around £73 and driving licences to around £69. Under the national identity cards scheme, our best initial estimates are that:

- a 10 year plain identity card would cost most people in the order of £35;
- a combined passport/identity card would cost £77; and
- a combined driving licence/identity card would cost £73 (though holders of both driving licence and passport cards would only pay the full cost for the first one they renewed).

In other words the estimated additional cost per person of the scheme is around £4 per person spread across 10 years.

179. The cost assumptions and cost estimates which have been used in the preparation of the Home Office's business case have not been placed in the public domain for reasons of commercial confidentiality. These estimates have been benchmarked with reference to comparable projects. Work is now being progressed to test the cost assumptions through modelling, trials and feasibility studies.

EFFECTS OF THE BILL ON PUBLIC SERVICE MANPOWER

180.   It is likely that there will be an additional staffing requirement for the introduction of a new identity cards scheme, primarily for the recording of biometric information. A capability analysis is currently under way with potential public sector delivery partners to establish the most cost efficient way of delivering this (and other) elements of the scheme, drawing as much as possible on existing resources. The programme of feasibility studies will also contribute to the evaluation of the requirements for additional staffing. No decisions have been taken as to whether any additional manpower will fall within the public sector.

181.   Any additional staffing costs when the scheme is operational can be met from charges under the provisions of this draft Bill.

SUMMARY OF THE REGULATORY IMPACT ASESSMENT

182.   The draft Bill imposes no regulations on any private sector or voluntary organisations, neither does it mandate which public sector organisations will be involved in the issuing of cards. There is therefore no meaningful regulatory impact assessment which can be published at this stage.

ECHR

183.   Section 19 of the Human Rights Act 1998 requires the Minister in charge of a Bill in either House of Parliament to make a statement about the compatibility of the provision of the Bill with the Convention.

184.   The Government does not believe that there is anything in the draft Bill that conflicts with the Convention and will prevent such a statement being made.

COMMENCEMENT

185.   Arrangements to be confirmed.

Annex C

Regulatory and Race Equality Impact Assessments

Regulatory Impact

1. The draft Bill imposes no regulations on any private sector or voluntary organisations, neither does it mandate which public sector organisations will be involved in the issuing of cards. It is not therefore appropriate to publish a regulatory impact assessment for the scheme.

2. As more specific decisions are taken on how the scheme will be delivered and used, regulatory impact assessments will be published. It is envisaged that over time this would include:

    (i)   the impact on employers of using the scheme for checking eligibility for employment. As stated above there is no provision in the draft Bill which requires such checks or provides for secondary legislation to be made requiring such checks. The relevant powers already exist under section 8 of the Asylum and Immigration Act 1996, though the Government will not consider laying new orders under this Act to take account of the identity cards scheme until closer to the date of implementation of the scheme. If revised regulations are laid, these will be subject to a regulatory impact assessment and full consultation with employers. However the Government will continue its discussions with employers' organisations and trade unions to ensure that employers' needs are taken into account during the design of the scheme;

    (ii) the impact on the financial services industry. A large proportion of losses to the economy due to identity fraud fall on the industry. Checks of the cards scheme will benefit the industry. However there is no requirement in the draft Bill for such checks and the draft Bill requires that all checks made by private sector organisations can only be made with the consent of the individual card holder;

(iii) impact on any private sector organisations affected by Clause 11. This provision in the Bill places organisations prescribed by the Secretary of State under a duty to provide information to help ensure the accuracy of information on the Register. It is possible that as the scheme is designed, requirements for private sector organisations to provide information may be identified. However it is likely that in most cases, these organisations will be in the business of providing such information, for example credit reference agencies, and therefore the issue of a regulatory burden will not arise. As the draft Bill provides for each "data sharing gateway" established under these provisions to be approved by Parliament, if in certain circumstances there is a regulatory impact on the organisation or sector concerned this will be assessed when the regulations are being developed.

Race Equality Impact

3.   This assessment has been produced in accordance with obligations for developing new policy under the:

- general duty to eliminate unlawful discrimination; and promote equality of opportunity, and good relations between persons of different racial groups which is set out in section 71(1) of the Race Relations Act 1976 as amended by the Race Relations (Amendment) Act 2000;
- specific duties in particular to assess and consult on the likely impact of its proposed policies on the promotion of race equality; to publish the results of such assessments and consultation; and to monitor policies for any adverse impact on the promotion of race equality which are set out in secondary legislation under the amended Race Relations Act;
- the Home Office Race Equality Scheme (in which the Home Office has set out how it intends to comply with the general and specific duties);
- Commission for Racial Equality (CRE) statutory code of practice, and non-statutory CRE guidance.

General principles of the scheme

4.   The draft legislation and the administration of the scheme is bound by the Race Relations Act 1976, as amended by the Race Relations (Amendment) Act 2000. Therefore, the

scheme must have due regard to the elimination of unlawful racial discrimination, the promotion of equal opportunities and good relations between people from different racial groups.

5.   The identity cards scheme will be an inclusive scheme, designed to cover everyone who has the right to be in the United Kingdom. It will show that everyone belongs to our society whether they were born here, have chosen to make their home here or are just staying for a while to study or work. It will help people prove their identity to access services such as free health treatment or benefits and give everyone confidence that legal migration will not result in increased fraudulent use of hard-pressed public services. If our communities have confidence in our immigration controls, they will be more welcoming of new arrivals, helping to promote a more cohesive society.

6.   The identity cards scheme itself is non- discriminatory as it is intended to cover everyone in the United Kingdom for longer than a specified period (3 months). The scheme will not, in general, require people to obtain a specific, additional document as it will be designed to make use of existing documents that will be **designated** as identity cards. Most members of the identity cards "family" will be enhanced versions of **existing identity documents** which are very widely held familiar documents that are already used as proof of identity.

Issues identified for impact assessment

7.   In preparing issues to be taken into account, we have taken the views of some members of the Race Equality Advisory Panel and other interested groups/ individuals, including the CRE, via two workshops, as well as views expressed by the general public and other organisations during the course of the consultation period and in the intervening period.

8.   We have also drawn on the results of focus group work and polling of black and minority ethnic groups, as summarised in **Identity Cards – A Summary of Findings from the Consultation Exercise on Entitlement Cards and Identity Fraud CM 6019**. This is very much a **partial** impact assessment intended to identify issues which need to be studied in more depth during the 12-week consultation period on the draft Bill. The main issues which need to be considered in the race equality impact assessment are:

(i)   the use of the card scheme by the Police;

(ii) how the general administration of the scheme will need to take account of the specific needs of black and minority ethnic groups;

(iii) use of the scheme in relation to public services and employment.

It should be noted that in the research during the consultation exercise, the concerns of members of the black and minority ethnic groups largely mirrored those of the white population e.g. whether the scheme would hold personal information securely. Concerns over the potential discriminatory effects of the scheme were secondary.

Police use of the scheme

9.   The draft Bill makes no changes to police powers and there is a specific prohibition on introducing regulations which would require a card to be carried at all times. The police generally have no powers to require a person to provide them with information about their identity. Police already have the power to stop and search members of the public under a number of pieces of legislation. Under section 25 of the Police and Criminal Evidence Act 1984, a constable may arrest a person on suspicion of committing an offence, which would not normally be subject to powers of arrest, if the identity of the person cannot be readily ascertained or there are reasonable grounds for doubting whether the name and address provided by the person are genuine. There are equivalent powers in Northern Ireland and similar powers in Scotland under the Article 27 of the Police and Criminal Evidence Act (Northern Ireland) Order 1989 and the Criminal Justice (Scotland) Act 1980 respectively.

10.   The draft Bill specifies the information which may be recorded on the National Identity Register. It does not allow for the recording of ethnicity. The Register will hold individuals' confirmed identity information securely and an audit of checks made of the Register, whether via an ID card or otherwise, will be held on the database to comply with the Data Protection Act. Disclosure of the details of a person's entry on the Register and audit log records will not be possible without his or her consent other than as authorised under specific provisions in the draft Bill. There will be strict controls and independent oversight of these arrangements.

11.   The draft Bill also provides for oversight of the practical operation of the procedures for disclosing personal information from the National Identity Register (see 2.38).

12.   However, the real concerns expressed in consultation thus far relate to how the police will use the scheme **in practice**. There were fears that the police will interpret the legislation

around identity cards in a way that will discriminate against minority ethnic groups, with a strongly held view that the police will stop a disproportionately high number of black and Asian people and demand sight of the identity card even though the draft Bill provides no such powers.

13.   The Government's aim is to ensure that officers have the confidence to use their powers effectively to tackle crime, whilst promoting confidence in the use of the powers amongst all members of the community, and keeping the bureaucratic burden to a minimum. The introduction of identity cards will provide a means of reinforcing awareness of the scope of police powers both to officers and the general public.

Administration of the scheme

14.   The application process will need to take account of the different languages spoken in the United Kingdom and must be equally accessible to all applicants. It is very important that applying for a card is easy and sensitive to the needs of all groups within the United Kingdom.

15.   The information to be specified in the draft Bill includes the name, address, date and place of birth and nationality of those registered as well as such biometric data as may be prescribed. In the case of third country nationals, details of any limitations on the right to remain in the United Kingdom and any limitations on the right to work will be included. A head and shoulders photograph will be included on the face of the card. This has raised the issue of religious head coverings, particularly for Moslem women and Sikh men.

16.   Nationality will be included. As stated above, ethnicity will not be recorded on the Register or on the face of the card. There was a concern that the place of birth appearing on the face of the card could lead to discrimination but this information is already required on passports and driving licences.

17.   The level of information to be held on the National Identity Register and on the face of the card will not be significantly more than that recorded now for the issue of passports. Regulations around the requirements for the type of photograph will be in line with those currently in place for passport and driving licence photographs. Sikhs are permitted to have photographs whilst wearing the Turban for inclusion in British passports and that is also the case for photo driving licenses. The United Kingdom Passport Service exercises its discretion and respects religious sensitivities as far as possible. However the overriding rule (set by

international standards) is that the applicant's photo should show a full face and that all features should be clearly distinguishable.

18.   At some DVLA offices, Moslem women are offered a facility to go to a private office and reveal their face to a female member of staff so that their face can be matched against their photograph. The operation of the identity cards scheme will include guidance along these lines to ensure discretion and sensitivity.

Access to services and employment

19.   The Race Relations (Amendment) Act 2000 extended the scope of the Race Relations Act 1976 to cover the way public authorities carry out all their functions. It has a wide definition encompassing a person or organisation carrying out functions of a public nature including functions or services carried out by private or voluntary organisations under a service level agreement. The Secretary of State and the designated documents authorities involved in running the scheme will therefore be bound by the amended Act. Similarly providers of public services who might use the scheme for identity checks are already bound by the amended Act. There is therefore no need for the draft Bill to make explicit provision for compliance with the Act.

20.   The draft Bill would not **automatically** require the production of a card for any service and there will be no link between the compulsion to register on the National Identity Register and a compulsion to produce the card to access any particular services.

21.   There is no requirement on employers to check an identity card in the draft Bill (see paragraph 2 above). In any case, many employers already see it as best practice to check and record forms of identification when employing someone to ensure that they comply with existing legislation.

22.   There were concerns that requiring the production of a card to access services increases the risk of potential discrimination. People from black and minority ethnic groups might be asked to provide the card as proof of identity more frequently than white people which in some cases might lead to people being denied access to services to which they are entitled if they cannot produce their card.

23.   There were concerns that the cards will be used detrimentally due to institutional racism existing in public and private service authorities, particularly where there was a reliance on

discretion. A view expressed was that, in this context, a compulsory scheme would be less discriminatory as everyone would be able to produce a card.

24.   The Government accepts that a compulsory scheme would be less discriminatory but there are other factors which need to be satisfied before the scheme could be made compulsory. The draft Bill provides for a 'super affirmative' process before compulsion could be introduced.

25.   As with police forces, the education and training of public service administrators will be an important part of the implementation and development of the scheme. It is intended to establish an accreditation scheme so that only those private sector organisations that have been approved (including banks, building societies or airlines) would be able to make checks on the National Identity Register on the validity of cards or the registered details. Accreditation could be removed if a particular business attempted to misuse the service.

Annex D

The principles of the Data Protection Act 1998

1.   This Annex shows how the draft Identity Cards Bill complies with the Data Protection Act 1998. The lawfulness test in the Act would be met by entering the scheme in primary legislation as set out in the draft Bill.

> **The First Principle:** Personal data shall be processed fairly and lawful and in accordance with certain prescribed conditions.

> **The Second Principle:** Personal data shall be obtained only for one or more specified and lawful purposes, and shall not be further processed in any manner incompatible with that purpose or those purposes.

2.   Clause 1 of the draft Bill sets out the statutory purposes of the National Identity Register which is at the heart of the identity cards scheme. It also specifies the information which can be held by the scheme. The draft Bill therefore makes clear the information about individuals which may be held by the scheme, the purposes for which this information is held and to whom the information may be disclosed. Schedule 1 of the draft Bill specifies in more detail the information which may be held by the scheme. None of this information falls within the category of sensitive personal data as defined by the Act. The draft Bill also makes provision for a national identity registration number in Clause 2. This number will be treated as a general identifier as defined by the Act.

> **The Third Principle:** Personal data shall be adequate, relevant and not excessive in relation to the purpose or purposes for which they are processed.

3. The Government believes information which will be recorded by the scheme as set out in Clause 1 and Schedule 1 of the draft Bill, is consistent with the third principle. This information is required to determine a person's identity and residential status in the UK. The draft Bill does not allow additional information such as criminal convictions to be recorded by the scheme though it does make provision for additional voluntary information. Where there are provisions to request further information from applicants for example to check the validity of their entry on the Register, the draft Bill limits this additional information to that which is consistent with the statutory purposes.

The Fourth Principle: Personal data shall be accurate and, where necessary, kept up to date.

4. The scheme will comply with the fourth principle mainly through its operational procedures rather than via statute. However, there is an important statutory provision in the draft Bill which will help to ensure compliance with the fourth principle by ensuring that details are kept up to date. Clause 12 of the draft Bill places an obligation on individuals registered with the scheme to notify prescribed changes which affect the accuracy of the Register.

5. There are also provisions in the draft Bill which require a person registered with the scheme to provide information which the Secretary of State requires to ensure that there is a complete, up-to-date and accurate entry about that person in the Register.

6. Clause 11 of the draft Bill provides the means for the Secretary of State or a designated documents authority to require any person to provide information which could be used for verifying information about an individual in connection with recording his details on the Register and keeping them up to date. To ensure that the persons providing this information remain compliant with the Second Principle, the draft Bill makes clear that a duty enforceable by civil proceedings applies to any request. An additional safeguard is that any request for information which cannot be met under existing arrangements must be approved by Parliament by affirmative order.

The Fifth Principle: Personal data processed for any purpose or purposes shall not be kept for longer than is necessary for that purpose or those purposes.

7. Information on people registered in the scheme will need to be kept indefinitely. This includes information on people who leave the United Kingdom and people who have died in order to ensure that their identities are not misused by third parties.

The Sixth Principle: Personal data shall be processed in accordance with the rights of data subjects under the Act.

The Seventh Principle: Appropriate technical and organisational measures shall be taken against unauthorised or unlawful processing of personal data and against accidental loss or destruction of, or damage to, personal data.

The Eighth Principle: Personal data shall not be transferred to a country or territory outside the European Economic Area unless that country or territory ensures an adequate level of protection for the rights and freedoms of data subjects in relation to the processing of personal data.

8. People registered on the scheme would have subject access rights under the Data Protection Act 1998. In addition the Government will investigate whether it would be possible for a card holder to use his card securely to access his own record on the National Identity Register, to avoid the usual authorisation process and cost involved in applying for subject access. The Government will have to be satisfied that this could be achieved without compromising personal information, for example that another person could not use a stolen card to view another person's record on the National Identity Register.

9. The Government has a great deal of experience in administering large databases of personal information – including where they are administered by a third party under contract. The Government does not envisage any problems in the scheme complying with the requirements of the Seventh Principle. The draft Bill includes new criminal sanctions, making it an offence for a person to disclose information on the National Identify Register without lawful authority. The maximum penalty for this offence is two years imprisonment, a fine or both. In addition, the draft Bill also makes it an offence to tamper with the contents of the National Identity Register. This is set out in Clause 31 of the draft Bill and the proposed maximum penalty is ten years.

10.   The draft Bill does not allow for the transfer of any data on the National Identity Register to other countries or territories. Disclosure of information for the purposes of overseas proceedings is allowed by virtue of the Anti-Terrorism, Crime and Security Act 2001. However the draft Bill ensures that such disclosures must follow the general disclosure Regulations defined by the draft Bill. In addition the power of the Secretary of State to refuse disclosure which is also a provision of the Anti-Terrorism, Crime and Security Act 2001 also applies to disclosures from the Register.

Printed in the UK for The Stationery Office Limited
on behalf of the Controller of Her Majesty's Stationery Office
4/04, 65536, 168110